A Guide to Leadership

SPCK International Study Guide 43

A Guide to Leadership

Edited by
Titre Ande

First published in Great Britain in 2010

Society for Promoting Christian Knowledge
36 Causton Street
London SW1P 4ST

The author and publisher have made every effort to ensure that the external website and
email addresses included in this book are correct and up to date at the time of going to
press. The author and publisher are not responsible for the content, quality or continuing
accessibility of the sites.

British Library Cataloguing-in-Publication Data
A catalogue record for this book is available from the British Library

ISBN 978–0–281–06207–2

10 9 8 7 6 5 4 3 2 1

Typeset by MTC
Printed in Great Britain by Ashford Colour Press

Produced on paper from sustainable forests

Contents

Contributors

Titre Ande is Bishop of the Anglican Diocese of Aru in the Democratic Republic of Congo. He was Principal of the Institut Superieur Théologique Anglican and gained a doctorate from Birmingham University, UK. He is author of *Leadership and Authority: The Influence of Bula Matari Model and the Potential of Life-Community Ecclesiology for Good Governance in African Churches* (2009).

Dave Bookless is author of *Planetwise – Dare to Care for God's World* (IVP, 2008) and Founder of A Rocha UK <www.arocha.org.uk> where he is now Director for Theology, Churches and Sustainable Communities. Dave is an ordained Anglican, and is Moderator of the Environmental Issues Network of Churches Together in Britain and Ireland.

Sue Fenton is a married mother of three teenage children living in Wellington, New Zealand. She has a BA in sociology from Victoria University in Wellington, and a BTh from Otago University in New Zealand. In November 2008, after completing her ministerial training, she was ordained into a pioneer mission ministry role with the Presbyterian churches in Wellington. Sue is passionate about churches being a prophetic voice in their communities.

Esther Mombo, PhD, DD is an associate professor in church history, gender and theology at St Paul's University, Limuru, Kenya. She is also the Deputy Vice Chancellor (Academics) of the university. She has published worldwide in refereed and professional journals.

C. B. Peter, PhD is a senior lecturer in philosophy, research methodology, and HIV & AIDS studies at St Paul's University, Limuru, Kenya. He is ordained and an academic publisher and research consultant, with over 60 published writings in several countries and media.

Leaderwell Pohsngap lives in Northeast India. Since 2005 he has been the International Director of Global LEAD Alliance, a ministry facilitating churches around the world to train their own leaders for the marketplace at their own cost and in their own contexts. He travels constantly to fulfil this passion. Dr Pohsngap is married to Rivulet Lyngdoh and they have three grown-up boys. Prior to this position, Dr Pohsngap was the Principal

(President) of Union Biblical Seminary, Pune, India, for almost eight years (1997–2004). He and his family were also missionaries to Kenya for three years (1980–3). Dr Pohsngap holds a doctorate in missiology from Asbury Theological Seminary, Kentucky, USA.

The SPCK International Study Guides

The International Study Guides (ISGs) are clear and accessible resources for the Christian Church. The series contains biblical commentaries, books on pastoral care, church history and theology. The guides are contextual and ecumenical in content and missional in direction.

The series is primarily aimed at those training for Christian ministries for whom English is an alternative language. Many other Christians will also find the ISGs useful guides. The contributors come from different countries and from a variety of church backgrounds. Most of them are theological educators. They bring their particular perspectives to bear as they demonstrate the influence of other contexts on the subjects they address. They provide a practical emphasis alongside contemporary scholarly reflection.

For over forty years, the ISG series has aided those in ministerial formation to develop their own theology and discern God's mission in their context. Today, there is a greater awareness of plurality within the universal Christian body. This is reflected in changes to the series that draw upon the breadth of Christian experience across the globe.

Emma Wild-Wood
Editor, International Study Guides

Acknowledgements

As this book is a joint effort, I owe a debt of gratitude to many people. I would like to express my deepest appreciation and thanks to my fellow authors who have so generously made their work available for this book. I am very deeply indebted to them.

I would also like to thank Emma Wild-Wood for her unfailing encouragement and confidence which has sustained the writing of this book. She has stringently and courteously edited all the pages of this book. Especially, she acted as link-person between me and my fellow authors.

It is my hope that this book will prove to be of real help to students in colleges and Bible schools and all those who are in leadership positions, enabling them to gain a deeper understanding and a richer experience as expressed in this book. May readers of this book be encouraged to go on to further reflections and study at greater depth.

Further reading

Leadership

Steven Croft. *Ministry in Three Dimensions: Ordination and Leadership in the Local Church*. London: Darton, Longman & Todd, 1999.

Glen Johnson. *Leadership that Builds: Nehemiah, a Model for Our Times of Crisis*. The Philippines: OMF Literature, 1996.

Kairos Theologians. *The Kairos Document: A Theological Comment on the Political Crisis in South Africa*, 2nd revised edn. Braamfontein, South Africa: Skotaville Publishers, 1986.

James Lawrence. *Growing Leaders: Reflection on Leadership, Life and Jesus*. Oxford: The Bible Reading Fellowship, 2004.

Discipleship

David W. Bennett. *Leadership Images from the New Testament: A Practical Guide*. Oswestry: OM Publishing, 1998.

James C. Hunter. *The World's Most Powerful Leadership Principle*. New York: WaterBrook Press, 2004.

Bill Hybels, *Courageous Leadership*. Grand Rapids, MI: Zondervan, 2002.

John C. Maxwell. *The 21 Indispensable Qualities of a Leader: Becoming the Person Others Will Want to Follow*. Nashville, TN: Thomas Nelson, 1999.

Prophetic ministry

Walter Brueggemann. *The Prophetic Imagination*. Philadelphia: Fortress Press, 2001.

Michael Frost and Alan Hirsch. *The Shaping of Things to Come: Innovation and Mission for the 21st Century Church*. Peabody, MA: Hendrickson, 2003.

Cheryl J. Sanders. *Ministry at the Margins: The Prophetic Mission of Women, Youth and the Poor*. Downers Grove, IL: InterVarsity Press, 1997.

Environment

Dave Bookless. *Planetwise – Dare to Care for God's World*. Nottingham: Inter-Varsity Press, 2008.

Steven Bouma-Prediger. *For the Beauty of the Earth*. Bel Air, CA: Fleming H. Revell Co., 2001.

Introduction: The leadership challenge today

This book contains contributions from church leaders round the globe on what they believe make good Christian-leadership qualities. You might be reading this book because you are, or will be, in a leadership position in your church. Before you begin reading the book, start thinking about the following questions and discussing them with others.

- Think about leaders where you live. What are they like?
- Make a list of qualities that describe your political leaders, your community leaders, your church leaders.
- What are the things that influence them? Are there structures and expectations within society that leaders feel they have to live up to?
- Can you think of situations in which some leaders wanted to work for good but they were held back by the social system or other people? List the influences in this situation.
- Try to understand why this happened and how it could have been prevented. This is called analysis. It is important that we try to analyse our own situation and discern how God may be calling us to transform it.

Now read this letter. It's written by a church member in Congo who is concerned about the quality of leadership in his church. It presents his analysis of the situation.

Dear Pastor John,

Thank you for asking about my views on leadership in our local church in Congo. Managing my business has given me plenty of opportunity to think about leadership so I hope you don't mind me being frank with my opinion and expectations. I strongly believe that good leadership is a key factor in the spread of the gospel. Good leadership is vital for healthy, growing churches. As leaders shape the Church for good or bad, leadership must make sense of a changing world and changing Church.

Unfortunately my experience of being led in our church is an unhappy one. Many of our church leaders seem to me weak, ineffectual, out of touch with reality and unlikely to lead anyone anywhere. Our leaders do not plan. They just let things happen. John, you know that lack of proper planning puts our leaders in the trap of reacting to crises rather than implementing pre-planned actions. Concerning ethics, they leave their wives and run off with other women, members of the church. They embezzle church funds for personal gain. They abuse their power and so damage those they lead and destroy trust in leaders on a broader level.

I despair at the lack of good leadership within the Church and I am looking for 'strong natural leaders', leaders who have energy, who are determined and focused. They walk with purpose and they thrive on action. They turn problems into opportunities. They work well with people, serving God together.

The other concern is whether leaders should always be male and ordained. Without doubt, lay people can have a positive influence, shaping people's lives and providing support, inspiration and encouragement in the Christian life. Surely, women are equally able to serve God as ordained pastors.

Today, in my business and in wider society we work to achieve efficiency, calculability, predictability and control. Don't you think that these insights from society should be adopted by the church leadership for the growth of the Church? I want to see leadership exercised in increasingly competent and professional ways in the Church. I would like to see 'fresh and imaginative leadership' within our church.

The inherited roles of ordained ministers no longer fit the needs of our present situation, so some rethinking is needed to equip clergy with the new skills they require. Shouldn't the Church look in secular models of management for inspiration, and for models for the role of the clergy?

I feel a growing awareness of the need for change. But our leaders must discern the direction of that change. As the futurologist Dr Patrick Dixon said, 'Either we take hold of the future or the future will take hold of us.'

Anyway, stay cool and thanks for praying for me.

Peter Kiongozi (Managing Director, Textile Industries Inc.)

Would you analyse your church leadership in the way Peter analyses his? Perhaps your church has different issues to deal with or perhaps you understand them differently.

Taking Peter's letter as my starting point I am now going to make my own analysis of leadership in the Church. I am influenced by my own church, the Anglican Church of Congo, and by what I have observed when visiting churches in other parts of the world.

 The problem

Peter's provocative letter to Pastor John raises many issues linked to the challenges that church leadership is facing today in many countries throughout the world. Unstable economic conditions and severe poverty lead Christians to look for competent and professional leadership in the Church. Leadership in the Church has become an issue of much concern and discussion among Christians themselves.

Many Christians think that poor leadership in the Church and lack of vision, skills and planning cause churches to limit themselves to the purely 'spiritual' aspects of life. Leaders take church services and visit their own members; they teach a limited doctrine of personal salvation but they do not relate it to the world in which they live. People criticize the Church for not developing a holistic ministry and not engaging in the world beyond the Church. They would like to see able and godly leaders bring the spiritual dimension into the community and the workplace, into politics and economics. Like Peter, many Christian business-leaders are dismayed by the mismanagement and lack of vision among church leaders. They want to make the churches as productive as possible, yet they see that leaders have no access to modern technological advancements and to the current secular principles of management. One issue that comes to light in this book is how the Church might benefit from the insights of secular management and leadership.

Perhaps, however, some people wonder whether change is necessary. They may think Peter is too critical. After all, in many countries in the world, Christians experience the wonder of worshipping in large congregations with vibrant music and dance. New 'charismatic' prayer groups and Pentecostal churches are mushrooming with an emphasis on healing and miracles. It gives hope for the future of the Church. It is also true that in contexts of hardship and crushing poverty, like the situation my own church in Congo faces, churches have been responding to human needs by loving service. They have been seeking to transform unjust structures of society – for example, working in the slums of large cities and speaking out against corruption, supporting sustainable development projects to safeguard the integrity of Creation, and working for reconciliation in order to sustain and renew the life of the Earth. Churches are often trying to serve their communities when few other agencies will help.

These different services have made the mission of the Church truly 'holistic', but increasingly demanding. As the churches grow, pastoring has become frustrating. Often pastors feel under pressure not only to produce growth in numbers but also to develop new programmes, to help more people. Some worthy projects lack the vision and coordination to be sustainable. Pastors are not sure how to make the most of their congregations. What sort of organizations are they? In what ways should pastors aim to make their congregations 'productive'? It is precisely the growth of the Church and the expansion of local congregations that make it important to look again at the characteristics of good Christian leadership in the contemporary context.

Unfortunately, most pastors were not trained to manage large and dynamic organizations or to develop a holistic approach to mission and ministry. Pastors attended Bible colleges, where they were taught to teach correct doctrine. The educational programme emphasized such subjects as homiletics, ecclesiology, eschatology, exegesis, soteriology and hermeneutics. Topics such as management and development have been added recently in many theological colleges.

The leadership values that have been most highly regarded do not always prepare a person for modern leadership. There has been an emphasis on unquestioning obedience in order to achieve a desired end, on discipline, hard work and self-sacrifice. Pastors have been expected not to show weakness or pain, but to continually display courage and endurance, and so be the highest example to others. While some of these characteristics are admirable, together they often produce leaders who are unwilling to share their weaknesses, and who do not like collaborative ministry or the sharing of authority. Those in leadership positions used to expect a certain status in society and to operate in a different social class. Today, societies are rapidly changing and are more concerned with the effective implementation of the leadership role rather than an elite group maintaining their status.

We have inherited a model of ministry that is no longer working. A growing awareness of this fact means that the need for well-trained, highly qualified leaders in Christian organizations is a frequent topic of discussion throughout Christian communities. There is a need to have better-prepared people to manage effectively the organization that God has raised up to accomplish his work. Change is demanded in the role of the clergy: new skills are required in the areas of enabling and collaborative leadership. Churches would do well to make use of the expertise of members, like Peter Kiongozi, who, as secular leaders, make leadership effective in the workplace.

Some churches, however, are in a different position. They have already responded to the changes taking place in their societies. They have been inspired by secular models of management and leadership, dressed them in Christian language and applied them to ministerial formation. The primary focus of what it means to be a pastor has become focused in the very exercise of leadership skills. Although the emphasis in churches is on signs and wonders, healing and evangelism, a lot of teaching in conferences and seminars concerns management and leadership concepts. Many Christian books on the biblical approach to management are valued as a practical guide for the manager who aspires to greater effectiveness and productivity.

Even though the word 'leader' was never used to describe Christian ministers in the New Testament, it is used more often now to refer to a minister or pastor in some churches. The Greek word translated as 'leader' in the New Testament is *archon*, a secular word meaning leader in business, politics or industry. Courses are routinely run in enabling the clergy to build up, encourage and support 'leaders'. This means that models for church leadership are currently based on the core concepts of secular management theory as applied to systems and organizations. The language used in these churches is one of vision, planning, skills, efficiency, calculability, predictability and control. Steps to building a healthy church begin now with vision and proceed to values, strategy and programmes. The models offered by these churches do not arise naturally from Scripture, but from commerce and industry.

Such churches embrace the insights of leadership and management by adapting them superficially to the biblical tradition. For instance, one of the churches in Congo has become increasingly rich by using commercial models. They have guest houses, shops, banks for investment and other commercial activities. The focus is now less on care for human beings and the whole of God's Creation, but rather on profit and efficiency. The wealth gained is shared among neither the leaders nor the Christians. Some individuals are making a lot of profit from church wealth. They have created a class system and consumerism in order to exploit Christians and society. Ministers have simply become the supervisors and managers of the system, ignoring the spiritual growth of their congregation. Colluding in this system means that pastors cannot speak or act prophetically by offering a critique or an alternative way of acting. In this situation the attempt to learn from modern, secular models of leadership has gone too far.

Of course, there is much that the Church can learn from good practice developed over many years in the commercial world or in the public sector. We have both a legal and a moral obligation to work within employment law and to conduct good practice in the appointment and development of staff. But we have to keep to the biblical principles of leadership. It is for this reason that Chapter 1 concentrates on these principles. Once I have laid out these principles a number of different themes important to leadership are addressed.

Throughout this book you will find criticisms of leadership models and suggestions of how we can be better leaders. Every chapter deals with a different topic and the authors have brought their own situation and experience to bear upon it. They have also provided suggested frameworks for action. As you read, think about whether you agree with the authors. There are questions at the end of each chapter. There are also reflection boxes through the chapter to encourage you to reflect on your own as you go along. Here's the first one:

> Make a note of some of the suggestions above and see if they can be applied to your own situation. Can you think of some suggestions of your own? Discuss your thoughts with friends or colleagues. Do they agree or disagree?

We analyse a situation. We bring suggestions from sources such as the Bible, history, custom, discussions with others . . . But we can't stop there. We must act. Once you have read the chapters, and have reflected on the needs of your own situation, it is time to act. The conclusion will give you further suggestions.

1

Biblical principles for leadership in God's mission

Titre Ande and Esther Mombo

Christians often criticize the quality of church leadership in one of two ways. Sometimes they say that it is not effective in today's societies because leaders do not understand the modern context. Sometimes they say that leaders respond to their context only too well and are in danger of losing a distinctive Christian element in their leadership. But when we want to know how God expects leaders to act in their contexts we turn to the Bible. The Bible shows a variety of leaders, some with common human failings. It also shows us the characteristics and qualities of good leaders, and assures us that by following Jesus Christ and relying on the inspiration of the Holy Spirit we can provide leadership in our contexts.

We will develop some principles in this chapter and ask you to think about them in your context. You will find references to other biblical passages in other chapters that will also help you build up a picture of how the Bible views leadership. Take time to look through the whole book and reflect on the different emphases the authors bring out as they address different topics.

The ultimate purpose of our lives is to bring glory to God and to participate in God's mission to the world. This purpose is the same for Christian leadership. We end this chapter by looking at mission in the Bible and asking how our leadership can help God's mission.

✳ The Old Testament

Leadership in the Old Testament begins and ends with God. Ultimately it is God who was the leader of the people of Israel. In Exodus 15.3 and Judges 5.4–5, and many of the Psalms, God is creator of the world and the nation; the Lord is a mighty warrior bringing salvation and deliverance from enemies of the nation. God is the ruler of all and the righteous judge. As judge, God ensures that there is justice within the nation, particularly for the poor of society. Leadership is therefore God's mission to his people. God accomplishes it by choosing human leaders.

Leadership in the Church, therefore, is based on *God's call* and works under God's authority. God called Moses for the liberation of his people from slavery in Egypt. God also called Moses, Joshua and the judges to ensure that his people were protected from the enemy outside the nation, who would regularly seek to conquer Israel. They were also to establish justice and right order in Israel. So leaders were seen as protectors and saviours of the nation through their courage and military leadership. They had to fashion the life of the nation around the laws of the Lord and administer justice within it.

The call of God to take responsibility implied faithfulness, accountability to God and care for the people of God. The divinely appointed king depended on God for help in battle and insight in giving judgement. In return, the ideal king loved the Lord and was both a mighty warrior and a righteous judge. For instance, Solomon, the ideal judge of Israel, was endowed with the great gifts of wisdom, teaching and interpretation of the law. But the rulers who were not faithful to the worship of the Lord and did not uphold justice and the cause of the poor were often defeated in battle. Rulers called by God had to be faithful to God and rely on him for any success.

Leadership based on God's call implied dialogue, the necessity of sharing and delegating the care of a large community (Exodus 18; Deuteronomy 1.9–18). The development of Moses' ministry of judging the people following the visit of Jethro was based on this principle of shared leadership and authority. Furthermore, the need for a king in Israel, seen in Judges 21.25, was based on the dialogue between the people and Samuel, then the dialogue between Samuel and God (1 Samuel 8.4–22). In 1 Samuel, God and the prophet warn the Israelites that kings could lead in a greedy and irresponsible way. Nevertheless, they agree to the Israelites' request.

It is worth noticing that the different books of the Bible also participate in a kind of dialogue with themselves. The need for kings in Judges and the warning about them in 1 Samuel show two sides of a difficult contextual issue. Each context calls for an effective model of leadership based on biblical principles. Kings are chosen instead of judges to lead Israel but they are still expected to be obedient to God's leadership. When Saul, the first king, proves unfaithful he is rejected and David becomes king after careful choosing, calling and preparation. There was a continuing desire to have the ideal king.

In your culture, how are kings understood? And how are servants understood?

Who would be the ideal king? Prophets called by God inaugurated a tradition of independent and critical commentary on leadership in their preaching and writings which continually contrasted the real and the ideal. There was a longing in Israel for the ideal king who would come to fulfil God's promise of salvation to his people. The ideal king was known in the prophets' writings as 'the anointed one', *Messiah* in Hebrew and *the Christ* in Greek. He was to be the hope of Israel. This expected anointed king was Jesus the Christ, leader par excellence. His reign followed a radically different model from that of the ancient kings of the Middle East.

✳ Jesus as leader

Jesus' birth is predicted as that of the coming king (Luke 1.32–33). He sees himself as fulfilling the expectations of leaders found in the Old Testament, the hoped-for Messiah. He is the anointed king, but his kingdom is not of this world (John 18.36), and not established by force. He is 'the one who saves'. The victory is won through suffering and death on the cross.

He is the teacher, the lawgiver, the rabbi and scribe, and delivers new laws. He authenticates his gospel through suffering and pronounces messages from God. Indeed, the biblical writers inverted the popular idea of leaders as powerful kings, and suggested that Jesus led as a servant. They used some of the prophecies in Isaiah (e.g. 53.10–11) to describe someone who seemed weak, having little authority or control, yet who had the inner strength of godly love, grace and wisdom that drew others to him (Philippians 2.3–11).

He teaches as one having authority, not as the teachers of the law (Mark 1.22). These other teachers presumably focused on rules and precedent, leading to more subtle distinctions and regulations that frequently left ordinary people bewildered. Jesus cut through this with clarity and authority. He focused, not on ritual cleanness, but on the uncleanness that comes from people's thoughts (Mark 7.14–23). Jesus challenged some wrong understanding of the biblical knowledge of his time. Rather than worrying about precise observance of the Sabbath, Jesus used this day to heal people, teaching that it was for human blessing, not religious bondage (Mark 2.23–3.6). And 'love your neighbour' did not excuse people from not loving anyone else. Instead Jesus' call was to 'love your enemies' (Matthew 5.43–48).

Some people would say that Jesus' style of leadership was the antithesis of modern, secular styles of leadership. Jesus was not opposed to all rules and regulations of his time. He was looking for a 'righteousness' that 'surpasses that of the Pharisees and the teachers of the law' (Matthew 5.20). He was getting behind the rules to the deeper motivations of the heart, replacing mere external regulations with searching spiritual principles, desiring new attitudes and values deep within the heart. Leadership today must go to deeper motivations behind the 'usual' rules, avoiding a mere repetition of the biblical principles without applying them effectively and wisely in today's world.

To be a follower of Jesus is to recognize his unique authority. It involves adopting some form of personal loyalty to Jesus himself. To follow Jesus is costly: his followers must 'take up their cross daily' and 'deny' themselves (Luke 9.23, NIVI). The followers expect, as Jesus did, rejection, 'persecutions' (Mark 10.30) and being 'hated' for his 'name's sake' (Mark 13.13, RSV). Then they will be ones to be 'blessed' in God's sight (Matthew 5.1–12).

Jesus repudiates titles and honour; he has harsh warnings for those who consider themselves to be teachers. Jesus' message is one of justice, judgement and the right ordering of the whole of society, beginning with the new community he calls into being, the Church. Jesus also challenges the use of power among the secular and religious leaders of his age; he repudiates both their attitudes and their methods (Matthew 7.29). He rebukes those in power without fear or favour. The least important in society is to be the most valued in the kingdom of God; whoever 'wants to be first . . . must be the very last, and the servant of all' (Mark 9.35).

How could Jesus be both a king and a servant? Should this be an example for us?

Furthermore, Jesus Christ commissioned, enabled and equipped his disciples for ministry. He took time with his disciples, both men and women, who accompanied and watched him at work (Luke 8.1–3). Twelve and then 70 disciples are sent on missions that were followed by reporting, reflection and learning.

Jesus also watched over the progress, vision and unity of the small community he formed, of course. From the disciples Jesus intentionally formed an intimate group of Peter, James and John, within the large group of 12. This was done not to encourage discrimination within the groups, but to build a small strong team as a pillar for the wider community. Pressure around Jesus did not deflect him from his mission. For instance, when Simon and the crowds wanted to bring him back to Capernaum (Mark 1.36–37), Jesus kept his vision of going on to other towns and preaching there, despite the cultural and religious tensions that existed between peoples. Jesus maintained his vision, for that is why he came (Mark 1.38).

Why did Jesus work with others? How did they help his ministry?

Jesus watched over others, but also over himself. He had a prayerful attitude to express his closeness to the Father. Some time into his public ministry, Jesus took a break from the crowds and 'went up on a mountainside' (Mark 3.13) to spend time alone with God (Luke 6.12). He had the discipline of solitary prayer away from the busyness of the community.

To lead faithfully, Jesus himself had to be led. He talked to his Father before making any significant decision. For instance, he talked with his Father all night before confirming that a particular person was the right choice as one of the 12 among the disciples. This has an implication for our ministry. When deciding who to develop as leaders, we need to spend time in prayer and be very aware of our own prejudices, such as gender, class, physical appearance, disability, educational background, skin colour and previous experience. We must pray and think in terms of people from all backgrounds and cultures.

Why did Jesus rest and pray? Do you follow Jesus in resting and praying? How do you care for yourself?

Jesus said, 'I am the vine; you are the branches. If you remain in me and I in you, you will bear much fruit; apart from me you can do nothing' (John 15.5, NIVI). Leaders must remain in Jesus, to be close to him in order to bear much fruit. Leaders must not make a show of their prayer like the Pharisee in Luke 8 who made sure everyone could see he was giving God the benefit of his attention. Unspectacular prayer carries us and holds us in times of turbulence and speeds us onwards in times of high pressure.

However, it's also wonderful to pray during pastoral visits or after other ordinary conversations. It shows that God's presence is the most liberating reality of human experience. If the leader takes prayer seriously, the congregation will ultimately take it seriously as well. It is worth noticing that Jesus not only spent time in prayer, but he also spent time in the homes of his friends.

How does individual and group prayer help your life and the life of others in your church? How often do you visit people's homes?

❊ Christian leadership

Jesus called, and trained for the ministry, 12 apostles, and later a larger group of 70 (Luke 6.12–16). The apostles then worked to develop the right forms of ministry within the churches. The book of the Acts of the Apostles even begins with the appointment of Matthias to succeed Judas (Acts 1.15–26) in order to avoid vacancy and disorder. Paul revisited the churches on his first missionary journey, appointing elders (Acts 14.23). His Epistles continually refer to the way in which ministry is to be exercised and ordered within the body of Christ, the Church.

The Church is the people of God. *Laos* is the Greek word for 'people' and the word 'laity' comes from it. *Laos* serves in the New Testament to emphasize that Christians are drawn from Gentiles as well as Jews (Acts 15.14). The term may also simply refer to the Church, as in Acts 18.10. Appropriating the covenant language of Exodus 19.5–6, the text of 1 Peter 2.9–10 claims the full title 'people of God' for Christians:

> *You are a chosen people, a royal priesthood, a holy nation, a people belonging to God, that you may declare the praises of him who called you out of darkness into his wonderful light. Once you were not a people, but now you are the people of God; once you had not received mercy, but now you have received mercy.*

Laos as the whole people of God does not make a distinction between laity and the clergy. It is a chosen people with a special status and dignity because of their relationship with God. To be the *laos* of God gives a sense of importance, identity and purpose to life. The free grace of God in Christ removes any basis for pride and contributes to a humble acknowledgement of dependence on God.

The Church is a unique community of faith, hope and love, called to be a community of worship and mission, and to instruct others in the way of faith. It was the coming of the Spirit that created the Church. The Spirit continues to give life to the Church and it is the life of Christ. God has poured out the Holy Spirit upon his people. Therefore, the Church is the community of the Spirit. The unity and equality within the Church comes from the fact that all members possess the same Spirit (1 Corinthians 12.13). Leadership, kingship and headship within the Christian community belong first to Christ himself, the head of the body, the Church (Colossians 1.18; 2.19; Ephesians 1.22–23). Jesus himself anoints and appoints individuals to these ministries, and these ministries receive recognition from the wider body of the Church. Any understanding of leadership and ministry within the Church must take account of our understanding of Jesus and his mission, the gift of the Holy Spirit to the Church, and our understanding of the Church as the body of Christ.

The Holy Spirit has given different gifts to different members of the body of Christ for the common good (1 Corinthians 12.7). Therefore, the diversity of gifts is to be treasured, but is not to be made a cause of showing greater honour to some members of the community in preference to others. On the basis of these gifts, different ministries are exercised within the Christian community for the benefit of the whole (Ephesians 4.11ff.). Secular leadership and management can offer through its gifted and skilled people useful insights to enrich leadership in the Church. Church members must therefore be allowed to use their gifts to build the body of Christ without segregation. In Romans 12.6–8, leadership is one of God's gifts to his people for the common good. It is the 'caring leadership' which is given through God's grace for the building of the body and the witness of the Church in the world. It is for ongoing transformation into Christ-likeness (Ephesians 4.12). We must use it with wisdom, a servant heart and a desire for the common good.

In Psalm 100.3, the Israelites sang, 'we are his people, the sheep of his pasture'. The metaphor highlights God's providential and tender care for his people, as a shepherd cares for his flock.

Across the ancient world, care, provision, guidance and protection were expected of kings as shepherd. Unfortunately, in reality, the 'shepherd' more often exploited the sheep than cared for them. Ezekiel vigorously condemned such shepherds and announced that God himself would take on again the job of shepherding his own flock. Christian leaders today must be good examples to the rest of the flock (1 Peter 5.1–4). They must provide care, provision, guidance and protection to Christians. Their duty also includes defending the flock from 'ravaging wolves', false teachers. They watch over themselves for their spiritual growth and over the members of the Church, as it is said in Acts 20.28: 'Keep watch over yourselves and all the flock of which the Holy Spirit has made you overseers. Be shepherds of the church of God, which he bought with his own blood.'

Think about your church, locally and nationally. Which lay people are actively involved in leadership? How can you encourage others to make use of their gifts at church, at work and in the wider community?

Jesus knew his calling and pursued a vision of what his Father wanted him to do. We too are called. Knowing both that we are called and what our call is makes a difference. As John 15.5 (NIVI) has already reminded us, 'If you remain in me and I in you, you will bear much fruit.' Those leaders who are called remain in Jesus and know that they are on Earth for a purpose.

If the gifts of the whole people of God are to be used, does women's leadership in the Church also have a biblical basis? Or is it, as some people suggest, simply an influence from secular leadership – an example of the sort of thing to avoid? You will need to consider the arguments and make up your own mind. For the following reasons, we believe women's leadership is vital for the Church and consider it at length here.

Women as leaders

Women leaders in the Church today are few in number and are often regarded with suspicion because of the way Scripture is read and used. There seems to be an assumption that leadership is masculine because public leadership in the Bible was largely male. This was the case in the religious sphere because all priests were male and came from a single 'chosen' family, that of Aaron. Other public offices, such as those of kings, judges and prophets of Israel, were nearly all occupied by men.

According to a certain rather skewed interpretation of some sections of Old Testament law, women were largely defined as minors in the context of the law. Economically, women were under the guardianship of fathers, brothers or sons who owned property, and were classified as the property of their husbands (Exodus 20.17). Women were expected to be subordinate to men and serve the purpose of giving birth to the men's children (Genesis 3.16). Women were isolated from positions of leadership under the pretext that they were unclean (Leviticus 15). When women in the Old Testament are mothers and wives – for example, Sarah, Rebecca, Naomi, Ruth, and Hannah – their depiction is positive. But there are other instances where the depiction of women is ambivalent at best. The interpretation of their stories depends largely on the reader. Some such women include Eve, Tamar, Rahab, Esther, Bathsheba, Michal, Jezebel and Vashti.

As far as Old Testament society is concerned, the larger picture is of women belonging to the private realm. There were, however, a few who became leaders in this male-dominated world, for example Deborah (Judges 4—5), Queen Athaliah (2 Kings 11.1–21), and such prophets as Miriam (Exodus 15.20) and Huldah (2 Kings 22.14). We also find a few women who were economically competent, like the ideal woman portrayed in Proverbs 31.10–31.

The Old Testament serves as a background to the New Testament in which we have the Gospels, the book of Acts, and the Epistles written by different authors. The Gospels, which largely record the life and ministry of Jesus Christ, show how Jesus related to women in a way that was radically different from the social context of his time. The different stories of Jesus and women in the Gospels show that he was aware of his social context and that he related to women deliberately in a different way. He seemed to challenge the traditions that barred women from taking part in the public sphere. A few of the Gospel stories bear witness to this, for example the story of the bleeding woman and the raising from death of Jairus' daughter (Mark 5.24–43), the story of the healing of the Syro-Phoenician woman's daughter (Mark 7.24–30), the widow who gave the highest offering (Mark 12.41–44), and the woman who anointed Jesus at Bethany (Mark 14.3–9). In John's Gospel, we have the stories of the Samaritan woman (John 4.1–42), the woman caught in adultery (John 8.1–11), and Mary Magdalene who was sent to proclaim the good news of the risen Christ (John 20.11–18).

If you look carefully at the encounters of Jesus with women, you will note that the women were carrying out the traditional roles in the private sphere. They were mothers, largely serving and nurturing the families. The women Jesus encountered were not in the public sphere, not acclaimed as priests, prophets and leaders. Thus in Jesus' different approach he broke the norms of his time, many times allowing even the unclean women to touch him. He singled women out. He had long discussions with them. He challenged the gender stereotypes such as unfaithfulness which, when practised by a woman, was a greater sin than when it was practised by a man, as we see in the story of the woman caught in adultery. Jesus challenged the gender discrimination of the contemporary world-view and interpretation of the law. He had a long theological discussion with the Samaritan woman, who then told her community about Jesus. In a context where women were relegated to the private and not the public sphere, performing stereotypical feminine roles, Jesus broke the stereotypes and empowered women. Jesus made society realize that all people were made in the image of God, and that God blessed both men and women, boys and girls, giving them power to manage the resources of the Earth.

Jesus came to this world to inaugurate a new era of transformation. But how did the Church continue with this? The book of Acts tells the story of the inauguration of the Church and the power to witness about Jesus. This power came to both men and women (Acts 2). This was a fulfilment of what the prophet Joel had said in the Old Testament. The coming of the Holy Spirit, therefore, breaks the social boundaries based on gender, class and age that existed in society at that time; the Church became a new community. It was inaugurated as a community that sought to do away with all oppressive social categories, and in the book of Acts we see examples of women who were actors in the foundation of the Church.

How can we continue to transform the roles of men and women, young and old, according to Joel's prophecy mentioned in Acts?

The first Epistles of Paul maintain the spirit of the early Church as a community that challenged the social and gender boundaries within society (Galatians 3.27–28). The baptism in water and faith in Christ nullified all the social boundaries and united all women and men into a new community of believers, which was the Church. The good news had set women free from the social boundaries of the time. In Romans 16, Paul greets a long list of women, which suggests a church community in which women held leadership positions, either independently or alongside their husbands. The list begins with the deacon Phoebe, a 'benefactor' of Paul, among others. There are probably two missionary couples: Priscilla and Aquila, whom we know also from Acts 18 (where they teach Apollos), and Andronicus and Junia (Romans 16.7). There are also other independent women, such as Mary who 'has worked hard'; Tryphena and Tryphosa, 'workers in the Lord', and others. Paul's advice to the churches in Corinth clearly presupposes a congregation where women are taking active leadership roles: 1 Corinthians 11 emphasizes that women should cover their heads when they pray or prophesy, an attitude which, in 1 Corinthians 14.1, Paul identifies as the most useful spiritual gift. This suggests that women were taking part in this ministry in leading worship.

Using the above analysis it becomes clear that the New Testament – beginning with Jesus, continuing through the Church in Acts, and right through the writings of Paul – supports the leadership of women in the ministry of the Church. But this is only *one* side of the coin. There is also another side to it where the same Jesus and Paul are used to deny women's leadership and ministry. This is what we will look at in the following section. We give the interpretations careful consideration because they are used today to prevent women from becoming leaders in the Church.

One argument against the leadership of women in church ministry is that Jesus chose only 12 men to serve as his disciples. The fact that Jesus chose 12 men as his disciples can be interpreted in two ways. According to the first, Jesus wanted men to be his main representatives. The intention of Jesus may have been to set up a group that represented the leaders of the 12 tribes of Israel. Since the tribal leaders were all male, the 12 disciples all had to be men too. But then it cannot logically follow that, just because the disciples of Jesus were all men, the leaders of the Church must also be male. This is for two main reasons. First, the 12 disciples are meant to represent the 12 tribes of Israel in a symbolic way, and are not meant to serve as patterns for the future Church in a literal sense (were it so, then one could even argue that no church can have *more than 12* leaders!). Second, Jesus did not come as the founder of any local church. Indeed, he is the foundation of the Church! The disciples were not meant to serve as paradigms of leadership for the future Church. In fact, their overall importance as leadership patterns is not clear. Some of them have no known role in the development of the later Church.

The second aspect concerns the definition of an 'apostle'. Was an apostle someone who had been with Jesus (such as the 12 disciples)? Or was an apostle a witness to the resurrection of the Lord (such as the apostle Paul)? Or was an apostle a messenger of Jesus with a special sense of calling, and carrying a special message from the Lord (such as Mary Magdalene)? This would mean that the apostles would not be confined to the 12 disciples, but would include others as well. And if an apostle means one who is sent with the good news of Jesus, then the Samaritan woman is an apostle too!

Then there are other ways of looking at the gender situation in the Bible. One of them is by employing the technique known as the 'hermeneutic of suspicion'. We can illustrate this hermeneutic with an African proverb: 'Until some of the lions become historians, tales of hunting will always glorify the hunters.' The point of this proverb is that anyone who writes history does so from their own point of view. They tend to include things that they think are important and leave out what they think is not important. If we apply this premise to the history of the Church, we will note that it is men who wrote the history of the Church, and the interpretation of the Bible, as they were the ones who had the knowledge and time to write. Male historians and interpreters relegated women to the periphery.

But we can recognize the significant presence of women among Jesus' disciples. Women come to particular prominence in the context of the stories of the crucifixion and resurrection. The Gospel accounts of the Passion of Christ clearly state that even though all the disciples of Jesus were men, it was a man, after all, who sold the Lord to his haters, and it was another man who denied him on oath, not once, but three times! And finally, all the rest of them – tough, boasting, burly men – ran away in fear leaving the Lord of life at the mercy of the merchants of death. But what about those weak and insignificant women? The women did not deny Jesus, and neither did they run away at a dangerous moment. They stayed with Jesus and were even brave enough to watch the crucifixion (Matthew 27.56; John 19.25). These extraordinary women are Mary the mother of Jesus, Mary Magdalene, and Mary the wife of Clopas. We are given the names of some of these women because the Gospel writers thought that these were prominent women, and their origin is said to be in Galilee. Again, the first witnesses to the resurrection were women. It is remarkable that the Gospels present women as the first witnesses of the resurrection even though women's evidence would not normally be accepted in a traditional Jewish court! What happened to these eminent women in the early history of the Church? No one knows. On the face of it, it would appear that historians of the early Church are somewhat silent about the role of women leaders in the Church. But by using the hermeneutic of suspicion we can take note of the little hints and suggestions of the shadowy presence of women. We do not find women in the centre stage. They hide in the background, almost ignored by the male writers. But they are there and their presence has lessons to teach us.

Apart from the issue of Jesus and the 12 disciples, the other reason against women's leadership includes an interpretation of what Paul says in the latter chapters of 1 Corinthians, the books of 1 and 2 Timothy, and Titus.

We may begin with 1 Corinthians 14.34–35:

> *Women should remain silent in the churches. They are not allowed to speak, but must be in submission, as the Law says. If they want to enquire about something, they should ask their own husbands at home; for it is disgraceful for a woman to speak in the church.*

Similar ideas are expressed in 1 Timothy 2.11–15:

> *A woman should learn in quietness and full submission. I do not permit a woman to teach or to have authority over a man; she must be silent. For Adam was formed first, then Eve. And Adam was not the one deceived; it was the woman who was deceived and became a sinner. But women will be saved through childbearing – if they continue in faith, love and holiness with propriety.*

In the above texts, women are forbidden to speak in church, to teach or to have authority over men. The context of the texts must be considered when interpreting them. Towards the end of the first century the Christian Church imposed greater limits on women's ministry than before. The writings of Paul fit well into a developing pattern of the institutional Church in which the flexible patterns of early leadership hardened into the threefold ministry of bishop, presbyter (elder) and deacon. Together with this the Church had gradually lost its radical stance and had begun to conform to the norms and expectations of society around it. Graeco-Roman society was very patriarchal and women were identified in relation to men, as wives, daughters, sisters, slaves and prostitutes. Independent women were not known. In this regard the Church began to adapt to its contemporary society in its treatment of women, in its development of power structures, in its approach to wealth and property, and in many other respects.

The passages quoted above seem to depict a different picture of the Church from the one found in the earlier texts that we have used in support of the ministry of women. The adoption of Graeco-Roman codes by the Church meant that women were pushed back into the private sphere. The latter teachings contradict the spirit of Paul as expressed in his earlier writings. So how do we treat these texts? Several suggestions have been put forward. First, it is argued that some of these passages are not Pauline but a reflection of someone else's ideas. Thus 1 Corinthians 14.34–35 is thought to be an interpolation because this text appears to contradict Paul's teaching in 1 Corinthians 11, which is much more developed. The position of these verses (34 and 35) in the text varies, which is often a sign of an interpolation, and they do not fit well in their immediate textual context, interrupting the teaching on prophecy. But the argument on interpolation ignores the fact that these texts were adopted as canonical by the Church, no matter who wrote them.

In the New Testament we find two phases of the history of the Church with regard to the leadership of women. On the one hand we have Jesus and the early Church challenging the social boundaries which had relegated women to the private sphere. The new community of faith disregarded the traditional social norms of gender, race and class. On the other hand we find the later Church reversed the earlier model and identified itself more with the social structures of the time, which justified the different spheres for men and women, especially in leadership. So those who wish to support the leadership of women will use the model of Jesus and the early Church, while those who would want to deny women opportunities in leadership will use the model found in the Pastoral Epistles or in some of the later Pauline writings. Once again we see a kind of internal dialogue taking place within the books of the Bible.

What does your church think about women leaders? What biblical passages do they use to support their view?

Leadership in mission

How does our understanding of leadership help us, the people of God, to carry out God's mission in the world?

To answer this question, we first need to understand what we mean by mission. Mission starts in the very nature of God. It means God's being is mission. 'Mission' comes from the word 'send'. God, as Father, Son and Holy Spirit, is reaching out to people, sending forth his love to them and seeking communion with them. God is a missionary God and sends forth his son Jesus Christ and the Holy Spirit. God's people, the Church, are called to participate in this missional love of God towards all people. In this way, Christians are to engage with the world in which God has set them. Christ-like leaders are intended to be models of God's love to all Creation.

In Luke 4, Jesus recognizes that he is to lead a mission described as good news to the poor, liberation for the captive, sight for the blind, and freedom for the oppressed. The goal of mission is not just the saving of souls. God seeks to restore communion with the whole of Creation. The whole of Creation is included, and this means every area of life of every person is included. It is holistic mission. God works to restore the garden, to build the kingdom. Luke gives us the dual mission of Jesus: to proclaim the good news of deliverance and to minister to those in need. The responsibility of this dual mission has been passed on to human leaders called by God himself.

Leaders must thus proclaim the good news of deliverance, but also minister to those in need. They must have a sense of mission and commitment. So the mission of church leaders is not a simple evangelistic message of repentance and faith in Christ; it is a message that embraces the whole of society: poverty, captivity, blindness and oppression are to be confronted. The Church's task is not simply one of making disciples, but also of transforming the whole of society, as the living God of the Bible is concerned with all people.

How would you describe a leader in God's mission?

Thus, the Church has a message of the cross that inspires leaders to make sacrifices for justice and liberation. It has a message of hope that challenges leaders to wake up and to act with hope and confidence.

In Ephesians 4.11–13, Paul says,

> It was he who gave some to be apostles, some to be prophets, some to be evangelists, and some to be pastors and teachers, to prepare God's people for works of service, so that the body of Christ may be built up . . .

Church leaders have a big responsibility to equip God's people in the service of building the body of Christ. So they need to be empowered at personal, professional and political levels. Leaders in mission are effective if they focus on empowering, freeing and serving their people. They recognize the importance of each member being able to provide others with the opportunity for personal growth and skill development, giving them clear responsibility and communicating the significance of the job to be done. Leaders allow people to use their talents, ideas, insights and creative problem-solving skills. In return people give to these effective mission leaders power, control and recognition.

 Conclusion

Christian leadership must focus on proclaiming the good news of the kingdom set within a very holistic understanding of mission. It is a leadership to guard and guide the unity of the pilgrim people of God in a particular place, and to raise, commission and nurture others in Christian service. The Church's concept of what it means to exercise leadership is that ministers should make their ministry proceed from Jesus' model of ministry.

? QUESTIONS

1 What does Jesus' style of leadership mean to you in your context?

2 What other important biblical principles would you add to those raised in this article?

3 What does your church think about women leaders? What biblical passages do they use to support their view?

4 Do you agree with the official position of your church? Give biblical support for your view.

5 How do you manage your ministry? How do you rest after periods of intense activity? Do you make sure that your activity is punctuated by periods of withdrawal, to be refreshed? Do you go away to pray and to 'be' in the presence of God?

6 Does secular leadership have an impact on leadership in your church? What is your appreciation of it?

2

Leadership and authority

Titre Ande

✳ Introduction

Anglicans in Aru Diocese in the Democratic Republic of Congo (DRC) were collecting for a thanksgiving. In one parish, Mr Mafu offered a big, healthy goat for the collection. To everyone's surprise the vicar who received the goat did not pass it on to the diocese. He gave it instead as bride-price to his son's family-in-law. Mr Mafu was angry and collected his goat from the family. The vicar immediately reacted. Without consulting anyone he excommunicated Mr Mafu, not only from his parish, but from the worldwide Anglican Communion as well. The whole community was shocked by this action. Members of the parish committee felt this unilateral behaviour by the vicar was unacceptable and informed the diocesan offices. As a result, the vicar declared that those members too were suspended.

Here is a story of a church leader abusing his position for personal gain and then taking decisions beyond the remit of his leadership.

Have you ever experienced a situation similar to this? What happened?

This example raises fundamental issues concerning authority within the Church. In this chapter I assume that a Christian community, like all human communities, needs structure in order to minimize possible tensions. A healthy society cannot exist in confusion. Society needs authority exercised through proper officers. I examine the following questions:

- Are there any particular types of 'officer' that the 'society' of the Church should have?
- Should 'exercising' authority resemble contemporary political government in its shape and methods of administration?
- What is the relationship between the ministry of the whole people of God and the ministry of these 'officers'?

What is proper leadership within the Church? Where does authority come from?

I will begin by focusing on authority in the New Testament to draw out principles for church leaders. I will then critique the theology and exercise of authority that developed in the history of the post-colonial DRC. The Church based its understanding of authority on the model of a corrupt political regime of which it was afraid.

> **Authority** is power that is legitimized and institutionalized in a society or other social system. **Power** is the ability of an individual or group to carry out its policies, and to control or influence the behaviour of others, whether they wish to co-operate or not.

✳ Authority in the New Testament

The context for any understanding of New Testament authority is the sovereignty of God: God who created the world continues to rule over its history, and more recently has revealed the fullness of the divine saving power in the coming of Jesus Christ.

The Greek word for authority, *exousia*, is used 95 times in all the books in the New Testament. In the Gospels, the term often bears a negative connotation, such as 'lording it over others'. Gentile leaders are known for behaviour altogether unworthy of Jesus' disciples. However, it is a neutral term that can have positive connotations in other contexts. *Exousia* is the legal and moral right to exercise power that is rightly possessed. Authority and power (*dunamis*) are related but different: 'With authority and power he gives orders to evil spirits and they come out!' (Luke 4.36).

In the New Testament, God is presented as the ultimate, personal authority and the source of all authority. All exercise of authority in the created order is therefore derived from God and subordinate to God. The kingly rule of God calls for a radical transformation of heart in men and women, a conversion that amounts to following Jesus Christ. Jesus possesses authority not on his own, but as the Son of the Father. Christ said, 'All authority in heaven and on earth has been given to me' (Matthew 28.18). The Father delegates universal authority to Jesus. It is not based on Jesus' resurrection or his exaltation to heaven, for he had this authority before his resurrection (Matthew 7.29; 9.8; 21.23).

Christ is the source of every authority. He underlines the authority of Scripture which brings us knowledge of Jesus Christ, who reveals God and is the bearer of salvation. This salvation is, in turn, manifested through and constituted on the basis of the life, death and resurrection of Jesus Christ. Jesus exercised authority by curing sickness, exorcizing demons, welcoming the unclean into God's love and forgiving sins. He acted with assurance and decisiveness. He settled the divorce question (Mark 10.2–9) in a manner unthinkable for a scribe. He expelled demons in a way that demonstrated that he clearly had authority over them (Mark 1.23–28).

21

Jesus lived the rule of God. The message and the works drew attention to the rule of God, and not to him. There was no disparity between what he said and what he did. The nature of his authority was displayed in the paschal mystery where he laid down his life in obedience to the Father and for the redemption of all. Jesus revealed in his life, death and resurrection the love of God and the appropriate response to that love.

The proposed style for exercise of Christian authority in the New Testament is service. Service is opposed to any 'lording it over'. Service expressed something essential in the character and nature of Christ and in the incarnation:

Who, being in very nature God,
did not consider equality with God something to be grasped,
but made himself nothing,
taking the very nature of a servant,
being made in human likeness.
And being found in appearance as a human being,
he humbled himself
and became obedient to death –
even death on a cross!   (Philippians 2.6–8, NIVI)

Here Jesus' kingship, revealed in self-sacrificing love, placed him at the service of both God his Father and the disciples around him. Superiority in the Church demanded humility and could be no different for anyone who would later be his disciple: 'Anyone who wants to be first must be the very last, and the servant of all' (Mark 9.35, NIVI).

What can leaders learn from Jesus' model of leadership?

Thus, Christians have to adopt a different approach to authority from that of society around them. They do so because this is the model of Jesus himself, the pattern of both his life and his death: 'The Son of Man did not come to be served, but to serve, and to give his life as a ransom for many' (Mark 10.45). The principle of 'not so with you' (Mark 10.43) shows that we are to adopt a radically different approach to leadership founded upon service to the whole community. In the Church, all members share in the authority given by the risen Christ (John 20.19–23), and all are called to build up the body of Christ. They live their faith, hope and love for the betterment of all. Therefore, people in authority have been sent by Jesus Christ, God's beloved Son, and they exercise their service as gifted by the Spirit for the benefit of all.

How can we be humble yet willing to stand up to injustice?

However, the story of Mr Mafu, as mentioned in the introduction to this chapter, shows that churches sometimes fall short. They base their understanding of authority on the model of corrupt political regimes of their time instead of applying New Testament principles. I will give an example from my own context.

✳ Power during Mobutu's era

Church leadership has been greatly influenced by the model of political leadership in DRC, which has emphasized personal power and wealth as a way of controlling the state. This influence has had a detrimental effect on church life.

Mobutu Sese Seko, the former president of DRC, took power in 1965 after five years of violence and instability that followed the sudden independence from colonial rule. He said his aim was to establish unity, to reinstate cultural authenticity and to work for economic independence. However, Mobutu's leadership style undermined his public objectives. He saw the country as his private domain and used authority as if it were his personal acquisition. Mobutu once challenged democracy by saying, 'There is only one African chief and he rules for life.'

Only Mobutu could command the nation. Thus the nation's unity was sustained by his hierarchical, militaristic rule. The 1988 constitution stated that the person of the president is inviolable and that he serves as a symbol of unity. The president identified himself as the incarnation of the Congolese people and thus claimed automatic and unquestioning obedience, personal fidelity and service. Personalized power led to an obligatory personality cult. Mobutu frequently travelled through Congo, immersing himself in the cheering, dancing crowds who were forced to attend and show homage.

To maintain his power Mobutu used repression. If he suspected disloyalty among his officials they were immediately suspended. The officials in turn acted in the same way towards the people who worked for them. Mobutu's style of leadership aimed to promote his own individual interest and to manipulate and undermine the rights and freedoms of the rest of society. He did this through paternalism, claiming to be the 'Father of the Nation' to whom the children of the nation owed complete obedience. He gave gifts to 'good' children and punishment to 'bad' children. This sort of system supports those in power and oppresses the powerless. Laws become synonymous with the desires of the ruler. Those who desire influence or stability seek out patron–client relationships and maintain unquestioning loyalty to their patron. So the system is perpetuated throughout society.

Mobutu's system also made a clear connection between wealth and power. In Africa, politics leads to personal enrichment, and wealth has a direct influence on political matters. The rich are powerful; the powerful are rich. In Congo, political and economic systems are the same, for those who hold political power also make the decisions about the allocation of resources. Mobutu became fabulously rich by using the resources of the state as his own. At each level of administration, power is used as a means of gaining wealth, which becomes a gauge of authority in society. Officials who administered state controls used them for selfish ends and to advance their own supporters. Civil servants supplemented their meagre salaries by exploiting their position in government.

Can you think of similar examples in your own context?

State power in Congo requires personal loyalty instead of an observance of the law, and dependency and submission instead of social autonomy. We can call this 'proprietary authority'. How does the Church survive in such a socio-political context? In answering this question I shall give examples from the church in which I have been entrusted with the responsibility of leadership, the Anglican Church of Congo.

The Anglican Church of Congo

In the DRC, more than 65 Protestant churches, including the Anglican Church of Congo (CAC), are gathered in what is called the Church of Christ in Congo (ECC). The churches appear to have cloned the model of political authority seen in the post-colonial regime. They have done so because they think they can best survive the difficult political situation in this way. Influenced by the one-party political system, ECC leaders pleaded for a centralized, hierarchical and personalized model of institution. They pleaded not only for political leaders to be respected, but also that they as church leaders should be respected. These Protestant churches are naturally predisposed to submission and they voluntarily accept state power, no matter how it may be manifested. The ECC Synod expressed this submission to leaders in 1989:

> . . . the word of God and Bantu tradition teach us to respect authority (parents, socio-political and religious authorities). According to the Bible every authority comes from God . . . the national synod calls all Christians to respect authorities established according to Christian ethical and biblical teaching. The synod also asks all denominations to offer solid Christian teaching on the issue of the authority in the family, society and parishes. The synod finally recommends that evangelists, pastors and Protestant schoolteachers encourage respect for authorities in the church, in their campaigns of evangelism, their sermons, and their religious and ethical teachings.

The ECC chose to interpret the Bible in a particular way. This meant that it did not question the workings of the state but followed its authority blindly.

The CAC, as a member of the ECC, developed its understanding and exercise of authority in the same context. The Anglican Church started in Congo in 1896 and developed during a tyrannical regime that misused power to diminish the lives of people. It is an example of a powerless social group compromising to fit into the dominant socio-political group. The CAC 'strategically' decided to adopt the exercise and understanding of authority from the national political regime. There was influence from the 'mother Church of England', but it is the influence of the national political system that we want to concentrate on. The following are some characteristics of authority in the CAC which I believe have been contorted by the context. When they are compared with the New Testament passages on authority their distortions will be clear.

Church leaders believe they have **supernatural authority**, given to some individuals through election and call, but not to the whole church. Authority is a divine commission to preach the word of God, to convert sinners and bring them back under God's authority. Authority is also seen, not simply as permission, but as power. It is power from God, enabling someone to lead ministry in the church. Therefore the authority of a leader is understood to come straight from God and is not to be questioned.

Justified by divine ordination, **authority in the CAC is understood to bestow social status**. Authority is considered to be formalized power associated with position, function or legal designation. The parable of the man who gave his servants authority over his house when he was absent (Mark 13.34) is used as an example. It is interpreted in the CAC to mean that authority is the power to make the final and binding decision in all issues.

Church authorities are seen as hierarchical. A pyramid of authorities is constructed with God at summit, the archbishop next in line, followed by bishop, priests and laity. The structure is considered sacred because it channels the divine authority. The holders of office often regard themselves as 'holy', in communion with each other, forming a 'sacred elite'. This power that is transmitted hierarchically is independent of the congregation (see Figure 2.1).

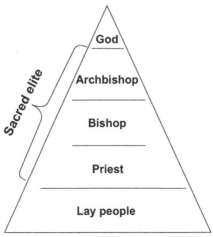

Figure 2.1 The triangle of authority

Church authority can become a coercive structural power that is inseparable from the person who holds a position in that structure: 'You are the
authority because you have authority.' In French, *autorité* means power, but
also the person in charge. Church leaders appropriate God's authority. They
can consider themselves to be 'God's representatives or ambassadors', vis-
ible signs of the invisible authority of God. Justified by divine ordination,
authority in the CAC is personalized and exercised through a patron–client
network. Consequently, pastors consider it wise to obey their superiors because their livelihoods depend on the good will of those superiors.

Titles used by church leaders indicate the sort of authority they think they
possess. The role of father as the first concrete representation of authority is
significant in most African cultures. The Church has adopted the 'fatherhood
model' in the same way that Congo's political regime was dominated by it.
In the Church the holder of a hierarchically superior office becomes 'father'
in relation to his 'sons' who hold subordinate positions. At each level, the
Christian family is unified under the leadership of its 'father'. Thus, respect of
hierarchy, order and discipline are believed to be fundamental in the growth
of the Church. When talking to a superior, it is polite to use the term *Baba
Askofu* (Father Bishop), *Baba* or Papa Pastor. Titles such as Son Excellence are
frequently used in the CAC. These titles are also used for political governors,
ministers and the president. Thus church members can think of their church
leaders in ways similar to how they regard corrupt secular leaders.

Amassing wealth is part of being an authority in Congo. The patron–client model of leadership has led to exploitation, corruption and suspicion.
Sometimes it appears that the Church's ministry has shifted from salvation
of the people of God to the maintenance of episcopal office. This has caused
competition and hatred among church leaders, with destructive effects on
the Church. The exploitative structural network is beyond the influence of
the diocesan financial committee and the control of the diocesan synod.
There is no clear account of church income and its expenditure given to the
community. Hence, Christians regard with suspicion the management of
church resources by local church leaders. Bishops often distribute gifts to
parishes after a confirmation service. These are gifts from father bishop
to his beloved children, who in return must express their deep gratitude
to their spiritual father. This practice has led the Church to adopt a totally
blind dependence on its leaders. It follows the state's strategy of manipulation in order to control all resources and be the ultimate distributor.

When leaders, religious or political, are under threat, they often use intimidation, suspension and assumption of guilt to track and destroy the
opposition within society and the Church. They take biblical passages out
of their original context and interpret them to support submission to their
authority. For example, in one diocese in Congo, there had been a serious
threat of division within the diocese since the year 2005. It started with
the election of a new diocesan bishop. Immediately after the election, two

unsuccessful candidates, backed by their congregations, expressed in a letter their well-founded concern about irregularities that surrounded the election. These two men were excommunicated by the archbishop for raising these concerns. They were accused of lacking submission to their superiors and the Anglican tradition. Romans 13.1–2 was considered a suitable passage to quote to them:

> Everyone must submit himself to the governing authorities, for there is no authority except that which God has established. The authorities that exist have been established by God. Consequently, he who rebels against authority is rebelling against what God has instituted, and those who do so will bring judgment on themselves.

Intimidation, suspension and culpability were used to crack down on this particular opposition. The two men were reintegrated in the CAC only once they had agreed to drop their complaints and submit to the authority of the individual above them.

Does the Bible encourage the style of leadership marked by proprietary authority, status and hierarchy as described above?

The words of Odette Kakuze to the bishops attending the African Synod in Rwanda remain challenging to church leaders:

> You who are our pastors, how many times have you visited the people who are poor, sick and suffering? Do you know where they live, the condition of their houses, what they eat, and the things they are in need of? Can you, yourselves, identify with their problems, the scale of these problems? Why do you make friends only with the well-off oppressors of the people?

How would you answer Odette Kakuze's questions?

Consequences

The attitudes on authority outlined above adversely affect the vast majority of lay members of the CAC. Lay people have been involved in ministry since the beginning of the Anglican Church of Congo but they are not considered to possess the same authority as clergy. Where an ordained person may be able to visit a congregation only a few times a year, lay catechists and evangelists take responsibility for that congregation. Nevertheless they are often seen as subordinates on the lowest level of the hierarchical pattern of ministry. Young people and women play a vital part in church life but because of a misunderstanding over authority their roles are not appreciated as they ought to be.

Young people meet for Bible studies, prayers, evangelism, games and pastoral visits. They sing in their choir during Sunday services and at funerals and weddings. Young people also work as agents of reconciliation. In the recent wars in Congo, young people developed a strategy for working with estranged groups. They have run seminars to bring together hostile ethnic groups and to work with rebel soldiers. However, very few preach and lead the service on Sundays. 'You are the church of tomorrow' is a common statement from leaders, based on the theology of age expressed in 1 Timothy 5.22 (NRSV): 'Do not ordain anyone hastily, and do not participate in the sins of others; keep yourself pure.' While old age is considered to be a sign of maturity and holiness, youth is seen as a 'sinful period' that can affect 'holy orders'. A young Christian very committed to work for Christ in his parish expresses the tension: 'The youth are very committed to the development of the parish, but they are only used by the church for manual work. They cannot stand before the congregation and preach or do the Bible reading because of their doubtful morality.' The integration of young people in ministry remains a challenge for many church leaders.

Even though the CAC recognized women's lay ministry from the beginning, because it fitted with the role women played in traditional religion in this part of the world, women's leadership is also hampered by the attitudes listed above. Gathered now in the Mothers' Union, women contribute much to making the diocese a place where people have joy in working together. During services, they take the Bible reading, collect offerings, pray, teach in Sunday schools, preach and serve as church wardens. They do evangelism. Women also learn practical skills, for self-development and to bring change in the local community, through small projects aiming at the holistic, social and economic development of each member. Women are used in different departments, whether at provincial or diocesan level, and they are represented in all church meetings. Women play a significant role at ecumenical level.

However, there are some cultural and religious forces that have destroyed women's self-esteem and made some people suspicious of women's authority in ordained ministry. Christianity has also made women's leadership a complex issue in the Church. Biblical passages are quoted and interpreted as evidence of the illegitimacy of women's leadership. Although a few women are now ordained they do not have access to all offices. There is still some uncertainty about their authority to act as priests and bishops.

Does the Bible suggest that lay members of the Church are inferior to ordained leaders? Or that one sex has greater authority than the other?

✳ Accommodation

'One body, but different roles' is a common slogan in the Anglican Church of Congo to describe the 'good relationship' between the state and the CAC. It illustrates the point made earlier, that the Church has adopted a policy of accommodation towards the state. So the Church has copied the political model of authority. A very simple example may illustrate this well. Church leaders enjoy the songs of welcome sung in their honour, as politicians do. They delight in a crowd of Christians waving flowers, and setting down their clothes for them to walk on. Nobody is allowed to talk to the leaders except through heavy official protocol.

It is this expression of authority that leads to the situation in which Mr Mafu found himself. His local pastor understood authority as outlined above. He believed he had the divine right to take decisions on his own and in his own interests; ordination had given him that power to reduce others to powerlessness in the church. He had adapted a Christian understanding of authority to that of the state to such an extent that the Christian one had become almost invisible.

The Anglican Church of Congo, like many other churches, models its authority on the state's form of authority. It is as if the Church is now taught by the state instead of the state being taught by the Church. This is a theology of 'accommodation'. It uses passages such as Romans 13.1–7 to provide an ideology to support submission to civil authority. An interpretation of these verses lies behind the statement by the ECC synod quoted earlier. How should we understand this passage?

In many countries, Romans 13.1–7 has become an endless slogan to back this submission to civil authority. However, to use it in this way misses the biblical concept that governments and leaders are ordained by God to ensure that justice is maintained in society and nation. So Romans 13 opposes totalitarian authority. It means authorities are given their power by God for the public good. In this sense, Christians are required to 'submit' to them. Laws are to be observed. But submitting in this context does not mean that every law must be obeyed. When laws directly conflict with the commands of God, 'no' must be the answer despite the consequences. The authorities themselves also need to be kept in check; otherwise they go beyond the prescribed limits of their authority, thus becoming oppressive. So Romans 13 does not automatically legitimize the particular style and laws of leaders, unless they fit into God's desire for peace and justice, not anarchy. A theology of accommodation to state authority is not biblical. Adhering to it has a detrimental effect on the whole church community.

Scepticism of authority

There is another attitude to authority very different from the one most commonly found in Congo. It is a view that is held in many parts of the world and it is important to mention it briefly. It does not follow the New Testament model either.

Societies like Congo show great respect to authority figures either out of a sense that they protect cultural harmony or out of fear. However, in many societies influenced by Western thinking, people have become instinctively suspicious of authority figures and their exercise of power.

They may think authorities are rigid and pledged to the mindless and insensitive repetition of the past. They believe authority limits expressions of freedom and thus prevents individuals from being fully themselves. They are often suspicious of inherited customs and received traditions as being ways of exerting control over others. Many cultures are experiencing a breakdown of consensus on ethical issues. The preferred ethical stance is to critically assess the evidence and develop individual moral autonomy.

Such suspicion makes it very difficult to appreciate the lessons that history and our traditional societies teach us about the nature of authority. The Church has been viewed with suspicion because, when cultural values are called into question, the value-bearing institutions of that culture receive the most criticism. The Church has also responded to some of these criticisms and is adapting its way of functioning as a community to the predominant way of thinking outlined above. Christians influenced by such suspicion can also fail to understand the meaning of authority in the New Testament.

Marks of Christian authority

The forms in which authority is exercised in the New Testament are extremely complex. Communities that were conscious of there being a period between the resurrection and the second coming did evolve structures. But other churches, in which the members expected the imminent return of Jesus, appear to have known little structure. Because we recognize the particular context of the New Testament we have to discern carefully *how* it speaks to our contexts. We work out which forms can most effectively represent the authority that Jesus Christ modelled. I suggest three marks of truly Christian authority that ought to appear in any form of Christian structure.

Christian authority emanates from God's grace

God has shared fully his sovereign authority with the risen Christ. Jesus now communicates this authority to his graced but stumbling followers by the Holy Spirit. Thus, Christian authority is understood in the context of the story of God's unbounded love and mercy. Everyone is called into the divine mystery as God's adopted sons and daughters. Unlike the understanding of authority often displayed in the CAC, it is given to all Christians equally and not downwards in a hierarchy.

Christ then, by his grace, calls us out of his love for people and his longing to fulfil his purposes in his world. The love of God is radical, costly and forgiving. God's love enables us to love God, and to love others (1 John

4.7–12). The Holy Spirit takes our strengths and weaknesses and transforms them. The Spirit uses them for God's purposes and for his glory. We rely on the Holy Spirit to empower and equip individuals to act with authority within the body of Christ (Ephesians 4.11–13).

This authority is thus an expression of the grace of Jesus, the love of God and the fellowship of the Holy Spirit. Christian authority depends on our relationship with God as Trinity. Leaders must be faithful to the Bible in all they do because God's word is 'useful', for teaching, rebuking, correcting and training in righteousness so that the godly person may be thoroughly equipped for every good work (2 Timothy 3.16–17). It is to be open to the Spirit because the Spirit of Jesus within guides and leads us into all truth (John 16.13–15). Our ministry must be sustained by prayer that expresses our dependence on God. This prayer responds to what God is doing in our lives and is the spiritual energy of our relationship with God.

Christian authority is service

Authority within the Church is grounded in Jesus Christ. Jesus' own exercise of his authority introduced a new 'faith-praxis' with a radically reformed understanding of religious authority. He used his power to confront evil and to challenge untruth. He acted in service to his brothers and sisters. He valued humility and included those whom society casts out to the margins. His saving and caring power was for the good of people. Therefore, the authority of all who share in Jesus is an authority only for the sake of service, an authority to care for others and to consider their interests. It brings salvation, as illustrated in the following case.

In a remote area of the Masisi zone, in eastern Congo, there was a priest who used his motorbike as an ambulance for the local community. The village was 25 km from the health centre. There was no road to get there, no car and no bicycles. The priest was the only person to have a motorbike. He used to transport sick people from the village to the health centre. Many people died before they reached it. The priest then decided, with the help of the local community, to build their own health centre in the village. Once built, the centre significantly reduced the rate of mortality. The presence and service of that priest were of great importance for the welfare of the local community in Masisi.

Christian authority is freedom

Authority also brings to people liberation from all that enslaves them. The Temple Cleansing Group offers a good example of this sort of authority. It is a Christian ecumenical body in eastern Congo. It believes that the message of the cross inspires us to make sacrifices for justice and liberation. It has a message of hope that challenges us to wake up and to act with confidence. The Church must preach this message not only in words and sermons and statements but also through its actions, programmes, campaigns and divine services for the well-being of people in the kingdom of God. For this group, the physical assault of Jesus to clear the Temple is revealing. He drove out the 'traders and overturned the tables and chairs that they used'. Of course, the Church's task is not to lead protests against any institution, but to support practical efforts aimed at affirming love, justice, freedom and human dignity. However, the Church may be irrelevant when it doesn't take action for freedom where it is necessary, as Julius Nyerere said: 'Unless we participate actively in the rebellion against those social structures and economic organizations which condemn men to poverty, humiliation and degradation, then the Church will become irrelevant to man.'

Christians are called to love their enemies (Matthew 5.44), but the latter must be identified. The Kairos theologians, who are critical of the apartheid system in South Africa, proposed such an approach. They said,

> The most loving thing we can do for both the oppressed and our enemies who are the oppressors is to eliminate the oppression, remove the tyrants from power and establish a just government for the common good of all the people.

Christian authority is communal

The Church is a community which arises through the common participation in the Holy Spirit that brings people together (2 Corinthians 13.14). It is a fellowship created by the Spirit, a Spirit-filled community. This fellowship transcends the unity that comes from being citizens of a nation, or sharing the same race or occupation or social class. The Church is the people of God who are now together in Christ.

The unity and equality within this Spirit-filled community comes from the fact that all members possess the same Spirit (1 Corinthians 12.13). Spirit-possessed Christians work in diverse ways that do not exalt one group above others. This can be understood from the biblical metaphor of the Church as the 'body of Christ'. It is about the close interdependence of the parts of the body. Each member has been given a particular gift for the sake of the whole body; and the whole has a duty to care for each of its members and nurture the gift that each has been given.

Therefore, any person in authority must enhance the union of all men and women with gracious God, and with one another in the body of Christ. The unity that the Church seeks is oneness in Jesus Christ under the inspiration of the Holy Spirit whose action is multiple, yet conspires towards this oneness. There is no distinction between laity and the clergy. Leadership among the people of God in the New Testament is never seen as outside or above the people themselves, but simply as part of the whole. Governance is essential to its well-being, but is conducted by the same set of 'rules'. Clergy are not 'set apart' by ordination. Instead their gifts are part of the Spirit's movement among the whole people. The New Testament does not value the individual above the group, as it may appear to some Western Christians. From the New Testament perspective, the community is still the primary reality, and the individual finds identity and meaning as part of the community. A greater understanding of this has encouraged the growth of lay training and empowerment in many churches.

Here are two examples of communal authority taken from different contexts. The Roman Catholic Church in Congo has developed a new ministry called *l'Apostolat des Dirigeants, Entrepreneurs et Cadres Catholiques* (ADEC). It is a committed group of people who have accepted Christ as Saviour through the Catholic Church and fall into one of three categories: political leaders, business men and women, and managers and executives in public administration and private firms. The first objective of ADEC is to train the members, through dynamic and committed pastoral care within the Church, so as better to live out the Christian faith in their professional capacity. Second, ADEC aims to accompany members on their path towards true and authentic conversion, deepening their faith and real-life experience of faith. Their motto is based on love, work and sharing. ADEC provides a model for others to follow in order to influence the management of national and regional public affairs.

A second example is the Transforming Communities' church model. This is a development of the ideas of the cell church and base communities movement. In the UK, for instance, small groups and communities are centres for nurture and pastoral care. They are also becoming centres for mission and growth in different ways. This mission includes evangelism, nurture and discipleship. These groups need freedom and the capacity to continue to grow in the truth and to multiply. Each member of the church who participates in one of the small communities is fully involved in living out the mission of God according to their gifts and vocation with the support and encouragement of a committed group of Christians. The groups come together on Sundays to worship and celebrate, but meet in homes during the week to encourage and enable one another in mission. The experience of the world Church suggests that there are virtually no limits to the growth of a congregation that seeks to express and develop its life in these ways. Ministers in this situation use their God-given authority to serve the Church by equipping and enabling these small groups.

What is the role of the Holy Spirit in communal leadership?

 ## Authority in ministry

If authority is a function of the Christian community and not a status of a few over the many, what then is the function of the special or 'ordained' ministry? The principal purpose of a special or 'ordained' ministry is to serve the continuity and effectiveness of witness to the gospel of Jesus Christ. Authority is not carried out as a personal right. Ordination shows that responsibility has been entrusted to someone who must answer to Jesus and to the community.

It can be described as:

- a service to the community
- always being exercised from within the community and on its behalf
- having no independent authority
- having no open-ended gift of power
- an entrusting of authority for a limited purpose within the fellowship.

Authority requires responsibility. A person who gives an order is expected to be caring and responsible. An impersonal authority does not exist. It is assumed that the authoritative voice means what it says and cares about what it asks another to do. People who are distant, uncaring and irresponsible about the consequences of commands significantly diminish their real authority. The best authorities are open, speak their minds out loud, reveal their purposes and do not hold things back. They make others take part in the decision-making process.

Ministers must keep a good balance in the ministry between deacon, presbyter and bishop.

- The right number of deacons ensures that the ministry proceeds from an attitude of service to the members; Christian leadership can be seen to involve many basic and practical tasks.
- A good balance of presbyters brings focus to the service of the word and the sacraments.
- The episcopal or 'oversight' dimension of ministry emphasizes the need to guide the pilgrim people of God in unity and to raise, commission and nurture others in Christian service.

Church leaders are commissioned to build the unity of God's holy, universal and apostolic people, and so set them free to engage with the world around them. They vow to guard the apostolic faith. As witness to the 'faith once delivered to the saints', church leaders are expected to be more than guardians, intent on preserving orthodoxy; they are looked upon as teachers who are able to bring the Scriptures and creeds of the Church to life in the present day. In licensing clergy and lay workers, the bishops or other leaders signify that those whom they license are faithful ministers of the word. They must, therefore, be well equipped theologically for this ministry of teaching. This then can lead to focused preaching that teaches biblical truth and encourages joyous Christian living, dedication, initiative and committed service for Christ.

✳ Working as one body

God in his goodness has already given to the Church the resources it needs to be God's people, and to live and work to his praise and glory. Thus, God has given the Church various gifts, to be used in love for the good of the whole, including the gift of leadership. The Church has to recognize the many diverse gifts graciously given to God's people, to be used co-operatively to his glory and for the salvation of humanity. Although the office of the overseer is personal, because it is a God-given responsibility to the individual, it is nevertheless also *collegial*. It is communal in an unbreakable relationship to the whole community of the baptized. As one report on ecclesiastical authority stated:

> The task of the Church requires the coordination of the many gifts of the Spirit, and a Synod is one way in which counsel may be taken and consent sought, and the skills and judgement of the whole people of God may be brought to bear on the issues and challenges of the day.

Thus authority equips and prepares the people of God for ministry in building the body of Christ. The authority for an individual to preside is valid only when it is accompanied by the common consent of the members of the church over whom that person presides.

The word 'authority' is regarded with suspicion because it is understood in the secular sphere to imply 'lording it over' other people. Authority is also suspicious because many churches in the world, including the Anglican Church of Congo, adopt secular authority that is exemplified by harsh regimes.

We currently live in a rapidly changing world. Change in our cultures has a significant effect on the way the Church views ordained ministry. Christians disturbed by change in every other area of their lives are sometimes resistant to necessary change within the Christian community and think this dimension of life, at least, should stay the same.

As the Church tries to increase the faith of Christians and to help others come to know Jesus, it is easy to abandon the biblical tradition of leadership. Instead, it embraces the latest 'new thing' without a critical analysis of whether it is appropriate. The truth must be sought in serious theological reflection. Our thinking as leaders should stem from reflecting on the Scriptures, instead of simply baptizing secular theories within the Church. Our concern is about the tendency of the Church to respond to the latest fashion. However, there is much to learn from secular insight into leadership.

Think about your own church. Do its leaders adopt leadership models from your social and political context? Or do they adapt them or reject them?

❄ Conclusion

The different contexts in which the Church has found itself through the ages have led to the development of different styles of ministry and of church government. This diversity has been needed. However, the example of Mr Mafu, mentioned at the start of this chapter, proves that there are some abuses of authority in the churches, the result of modelling their authority on the secular idea of 'lording it over'. Therefore, there is a need for the whole Church to reflect on, and develop its understanding of, the ministry of the whole people of God, and how that ministry is to be ordered within the body of Christ. We pray that, 'since through God's mercy we have this ministry, we do not lose heart'.

? QUESTIONS

1 Define the words 'power', 'control' and 'authority'. What are the differences between their meanings? Can you think of times when people have confused their meanings and acted inappropriately?

2 What connection between political and ecclesiastical leadership models have you experienced? Are they unhealthy, like the Congo model explained above? Or have you experienced some good models? What is the difference?

3 Who was Paul writing to in Romans 13? What was their context? How can we understand this chapter in our own contexts?

4 Explain what is meant by the assertion that Christian authority 'emanates from God's grace' and is 'service', 'freedom' and 'communal'. Give examples of when you have seen this kind of authority in action.

5 How does God's authority equip all Christians for God's mission in the world? In what ways does this work in your church?

3

Leadership and discipleship

Leaderwell Pohsngap

 Discipleship leads to leadership

Discipleship brings to mind the idea of being behind someone; learning from someone; following someone else or serving others. To be a disciple is to be a servant. Jesus made it clear to his disciples that following him means serving others, just as he gave his life for others. He said this in the context of his two disciples asking for a privileged position (Mark 10.35–45). I do not think that Jesus meant here that the intention of serving others must be to achieve greatness but rather that servanthood does lead to impact on both the servant and those served. Paul urged his readers to follow Jesus' example, who is the Lord of life, yet chose to be a servant of all (Philippians 2.5–11).

Discipleship is not something many people aspire to. Yet, it is the way to leadership. As many of those in leadership positions know, they became leaders because they had followed others. They also know that to be effective leaders, they must continue to follow others or follow certain principles. So in order to be a leader one has to be a disciple. Malcolm Webber was right when in *Healthy Followers*, he wrote:

> Everyone – including leaders – is a follower at one time or another in their lives. Most individuals, even those in positions of high authority, have a supervisor of some kind. In fact, for many people it is not uncommon to switch between being a leader and being a follower several times during the course of a single day. For example, in an organization, middle managers answer to vice-presidents, who answer to Chief Executive Officers (CEOs), who answer to boards of directors. Moreover, research on high performance teams has demonstrated that the most successful teams are those that have a great deal of role-switching among team members about who is serving in a leadership role at any given time.

Leadership conjures up ideas of position, power and privilege. People who achieve such positions are often called 'great'. Perhaps this was in the mind of the apostolic brothers, James and John, when they used their mother to ask Jesus for a privileged position in the future (Matthew 20.20–28). It is human nature to want to be somebody. The rest of the disciples were angry at James and John. Not because they dared to ask Jesus for such a position but because the brothers beat the rest in the game. Jesus did not rebuke them for their desire to be great. He chided them for thinking just like the world did. His way to greatness or leadership is different. His way is to be a servant. It is as if we can hear him say, 'Be a disciple first and eventually you get to leadership.'

The continuum

The relation of discipleship to leadership is a continuum that places a person on different points at different times. In Figure 3.1, where 'D' is a starting point for discipleship, 'L' a point for leadership, and 'M' a midpoint, any person is at a certain place on this continuum at any one time. Their position in this continuum is determined by age, knowledge, job, education and experience. The culture of the person also influences the position.

For example, in my Indian culture, age is an important factor in determining leadership. Youngsters in my world, at least in the past, have always looked to their elders for leadership in many areas of life. Elderly people in my culture will have a social standing at position 'y', just because of their age. But if that leadership position is determined by educational expertise, an elder will yield to a youngster who has the right degree. Thus an elderly person who is normally at 'y' on the social scale will be at 'x' in relation to a young person who has the right degree for a particular purpose. A person who has a certain position will always assume leadership, though he may be younger or not have a degree above others. The same person who holds a high-level position in one area may, in another area, become a follower of someone with a lower social rank.

This interplay of discipleship–leadership roles is played out all the time in real life. As an example, take Benjamin and Stephen who are close friends and colleagues. They work in the same place and attend the same church. Let us look at how their roles vary depending on the above factors by using Figure 3.1. Benjamin, a counsellor, is 50 years old, and Stephen, a landscape gardener, is 35. The two met in the church and their friendship grew. Benjamin is older and wiser. He is a leader at position 'y' and Stephen has assumed position 'x'. Stephen looks to Benjamin for advice all the time. Thus Benjamin becomes the leader and Stephen becomes the disciple. After some time, the church asks them to serve on a committee to improve the church's grounds. Stephen, though younger, is made the chair of the committee because of his technical expertise. Now in this new arrangement, Stephen is at position 'y' and Benjamin at 'x'. They play these roles interchangeably for many months, changing their positions depending on the time and cir-

Figure 3.1 Discipleship–leadership continuum

cumstances they find themselves in during the period (this interchangeable aspect is expressed by the broken line).

Influence

There are many definitions of leadership. Here are three, borrowed from many people:

- To lead is to influence and direct people to win their confidence, respect and loyal co-operation in achieving common objectives.
- The first job of a leader is to define a vision for the organization . . . Leadership is the capacity to translate vision into reality.
- Leadership is the skill of influencing people to enthusiastically work toward goals identified as being for the common good, with character that inspires confidence.

Do you agree with these definitions? Do they describe *Christian* leadership? Would you add anything to them?

There are some important operative words in these definitions. One is 'skill'. This is a learned and acquired ability. This means that leadership can be learned. Another word is 'influence'. Leaders are those who are able to make the most of other people, so that they give themselves, and all that they have, to fulfil a mission. There is so much power in leadership. The third word is 'character'. This word defines a person who is always doing the right thing. The issue is so important that character development is really the same as leadership development.

With these definitions, there is a new way of understanding leadership. It is no longer about position and power – or the privileges that might accompany them. It is actually about influence. And if by leadership we mean the power of influence, then everyone can be a leader. This is beautiful because just as everyone can be a disciple, so every disciple can also be a leader. Everyone can influence someone else, including those in positions above us. We can actually influence 360 degrees. That means we can include those over us, such as our bosses, our elders, our parents. We can influence those under us, such as our subordinates, our children, our youngsters. We can also influence our peers, colleagues and acquaintances. During a recent revival in the Presbyterian Church in Meghalaya, Northeast India, many elders took steps towards change because many youngsters, who experienced revival and thus were transformed by the Holy Spirit, confronted their elders about their wayward behaviour. In this instance the children influenced those considered to be senior to them. This is the way we think all the time when we talk of leadership. It is also true that we influence friends on the same level with us, neighbours who are neither 'above' nor 'below' us, and acquaintances we meet in many places.

To influence is to cause someone to act, think or behave in a certain way. The influencers have the power to do this because of their position, power, knowledge, skill or character. But for the followers of Jesus Christ, the influence comes from the transforming power of the Holy Spirit. Indeed without the Holy Spirit, no one can produce the sort of character that will influence the world. The disciples of Jesus were filled and transformed by the Holy Spirit and then turned the world upside down (Acts 17.6).

It reminds me of many years ago when I was a pastor and travelled to a small rural village in my area. One Sunday evening, while visiting some elders, we went to visit a family. Before we entered the house, the elders warned me about the father in that house who was a terrible tyrant. Sometimes when he got drunk the entire village would run away to the jungle for the whole night. He put fear into the heart of everyone and thus influenced the village negatively. By the grace of God, during that visit we talked about the need for change, and that night in the church he gave his life to Jesus Christ. When I went back about three years later, that brother was the one taking me to visit homes and everyone was happy to see him. What a transforming influence for those who experience Christ through him.

Leaders influence both negatively and positively. Negative influence uses mere position and power, which does not help people. When the dictator Idi Amin ruled Uganda, he could influence any decision he wished. But now he is dead those influences have largely disappeared. We admire people with knowledge and skills. Very often they influence us in making decisions. But leaders who influence positively and whom we want to emulate are those with character. We can think of Abraham Lincoln, Mahatma Gandhi and Martin Luther King. They had tremendous influence on their world and on posterity. All three were assassinated because some people hated them and their causes so much. But no one, not even their enemies, would question their character. Tolstoy wrote of Lincoln,

> Why was Lincoln so great that he overshadows all other national heroes? He really was not a great general like Napoleon or Washington; he was not such a skilful statesman as Gladstone or Frederick the Great; but his supremacy expresses itself altogether in his peculiar moral power and in the greatness of his character.

Leadership is so important and it develops from the inside out. If you are transformed inwardly you will become a good leader externally. People will want to follow you. Indeed there is no organization, institution or work in the world without leaders. If a nation has a good leader, that nation will prosper. A bad leader will bring doom to his country. This principle applies to the church, as well as to the community and family.

Because of the power and privileges that come with leadership, it is much sought after, even to the extent of using schemes or force to attain it. To be a Christian leader of influence, one must be willing to go against the grain, work hard and be open to continuous learning. In other words, leaders in the mould of Jesus must be his disciples first.

Think of some effective leaders you know. What are the characteristics that make them influential?

✳ The importance of discipleship

A disciple is a learner. This is the basic meaning of the word *mathetes* in the Bible. The first followers of Jesus were called the 'disciples'. They became great leaders but throughout their lives they kept on learning. They were learners for life while becoming leaders who would turn the world upside down. Disciples of other teachers expected to become teachers themselves, but Jesus called his disciples to lifelong surrender and commitment to follow him. Jesus spent more time teaching the disciples how to follow than instructing them on how to lead. Leaders who follow Jesus must know that before all else they are sheep, not shepherds; they are children, not parents; imitators, not models.

Discipleship is about serving by following in the footsteps of the Lord Jesus Christ, the suffering servant. He challenged those who wanted to follow him, 'Take my yoke upon you and learn from me, for I am gentle and humble in heart, and you will find rest for your souls' (Matthew 11.29). Jesus calls us not to strive to achieve, but to take what he gives to us, to follow his example of gentleness and humility.

Discipleship is about continuing education. We see this in the life of Jesus with regard to all his followers. He went everywhere teaching, healing and preaching (Matthew 9.35). Two-thirds of Jesus' work was education. Continuing education means continuous learning for those who want to be effective leaders. Jesus indeed told his disciples that they would carry on learning through the ongoing work of the Holy Spirit (John 14.26).

Discipleship is also about *unlearning* the principles and habits that prevent one from being a good leader. Paul had to unlearn many things in order to be a follower of Jesus Christ and become a Christ-like leader. Some things he used to cherish became worthless when considering how better to influence others in his new understanding of leadership. He recognized that he must share in Christ's sufferings as well as experience the power of the resurrection (Philippians 3.4–11).

One can conclude, therefore, that people can only influence if they, themselves, have been influenced. In other words, no one can be an effective leader without a willingness to be a serious disciple. Jesus did not call any of the disciples 'shepherd' until after the resurrection, when he spoke to Peter in John 21. Only after the disciples had learned to follow could they be trusted to lead. As a popular saying has it: the moment you stop learning, you stop leading. If someone thinks they know all the answers, they will stop learning and they will not be able to lead effectively.

✳ Attitude of a disciple–leader

A disciple who is called to leadership needs to have the right attitude. If, as we have said, a disciple is a servant, then an attitude that is necessary is a servant attitude. There are many ways in which this attitude is expressed. The best example of a servant attitude is that of Jesus Christ, as Paul recorded when he wrote to the church at Philippi: 'Your attitude should be the same as that of Christ Jesus' (Philippians 2.5). He went on to explain that Jesus is God yet he humbled himself and willingly took the form of a servant and suffered death on the cross in obedience to the mission he was sent on. Because of this act, God the Father exalted him and made him Lord of all, to whom every knee shall bow. A Christ-like disciple must have an attitude of service, of humility and of obedience.

Jesus has a goal to achieve, which is to bring salvation to the world. Although he is under someone else, a disciple is not without a goal. Every disciple must have a goal of leading. When Jesus called the 12 disciples, he gave them the goal: that of being fishers of men, meaning bringing people to the kingdom. In fact, to become a great leader some day, that is, a great influencer for the kingdom regardless of one's position and power, is a goal worth pursuing. Without this goal, life will be mundane and a drudgery.

Jesus was willing to start from the bottom in order to lead the world to God. Though he is God yet he came as a helpless baby, becoming weak and taking the form of a human being to achieve the goal for which he came. The prophecy about this is beautifully portrayed in Isaiah 53. In the prophecy about the Lord's goal, we see him as the servant of God, chosen by God and in whom God's spirit resides. His goal was clear and that is to bring justice to the nations or people groups, to open their eyes, to free people from captivity and darkness (Isaiah 42). He came with gentleness and in faithfulness he fulfilled the goal for which he was sent. The glorification of the Lord came with his obedience to fulfil his calling. This is a radical understanding of discipleship. To be great in the kingdom means to fulfil God's call. Many people over the centuries have left their position to pursue God. Surely the more they obey, the greater is the authority God bestows upon them. Paul definitely demonstrated this when talking about his past achievements,

> But whatever was to my profit I now consider my loss . . . I consider them rubbish, that I may gain Christ and be found in him, not having a righteousness of my own that comes from the law, but that which is through faith in Christ – the righteousness that comes from God and is by faith. (Philippians 3.7–9)

Once Paul decided to become a disciple, he left all his positions of power and started from the bottom. God glorified him so much that he became one of the persons with greater divine authority.

The incarnation is still a mystery because we will never understand how God remained fully God and yet became a real human being. In the same sense that we will never understand the depth of incarnation, we will never be able to explain its purpose fully. My former seminary president, Dr Athyal from India, wrote this reflection this year that challenged me deeply.

> The cross is the meeting place of God's justice/wrath and his limitless love and it is immensely much more. In the nature and ministry of Jesus Christ there is a basic inner bond and interworking of two seemingly contrasting aspects:
>
> - He establishes his kingdom through the totally unexpected way of the cross.
> - The King, the lion of Judah, is the slain lamb.
> - The one who triumphantly enters Jerusalem on a Sunday is crucified that Friday.
> - The Lord and Master washes the feet of his disciples like a servant.
> - The judge of all judges and peoples submits himself to be unjustly judged.
> - The crucifixion of Jesus is described as his glorification (John 12.23; 13.31).

The coming together of these polar extremes is seen throughout the life of Jesus. The one who is 'born the king of the Jews' shared his birth site with cattle. The one who created and owned everything had to be born and buried in borrowed places, and during his ministry did not have a place to lay down his head. He taught that those who follow him should deny themselves, take up the cross and follow him. He said, 'One who wants to be first must be the very last and servant of all.' To find life one should lose it. Self-emptying is the only way to be filled. True power is in powerlessness, as God's strength 'is made perfect in weakness' (2 Corinthians 12.9).

Did God become human to understand human struggles and sufferings? Did God become human that humans can understand him? Whatever it may be, in incarnation, God connects with those for whom he came. This is more than building relationships, though that is part of it. It is empathizing with those in need. Jesus was connected to his earthly family as a child. The first miracle was performed on the request of his mother. Upon the cross, he was so concerned for Mary that he asked John the disciple to take care of her. He connected to his disciples. The very purpose of calling them was that first they must be with him in communion before he sent them out to minister (Mark 3.14). He connected to the children and urged the disciples to allow the children to come to him. He was connected to the woman at the well and led her from being the most despised woman in town to the most enthusiastic evangelist. He connected with the sick, the lame and the blind. He connected with the bereaved in order to glorify God. This he plainly explained when Lazarus died. The connection was so deep that Jesus wept. The principle of connectivity or identifying with the needy is indispensable for any disciple who wants to be a great leader.

The suffering that Jesus went through to fulfil his mission was incredible. Perhaps no human being could tolerate it: the opposition, the poverty, the physical stress, rejection and betrayal were real. But Jesus was committed to the end. He was willing to pay the price. When the heaviness of the cross was upon him, he did pray to the Father that he might be rid of it. But in the same breath he said, 'not my will but yours' (Luke 22.42). This is the spirit of commitment and he gave up his life for it. In striving towards the goal of leadership, or influencing people in the values of the kingdom, a disciple needs commitment to stay the course. There are many challenges and in real life many fall by the wayside. Perhaps this is one reason why there are so few leaders who get to the top level of Christian leadership. Those few are willing to pay the price but the majority fail.

What enabled Jesus to suffer, stay the course and fulfil his mission? I believe it was an attitude of humility. Paul said in the Philippians text, 'he humbled himself' (2.8). He intentionally took the position of a servant. He is God but he made himself a servant. This attitude of humility has made many great leaders engrave their names in the pages of history. Take Paul, for example, the greatest of spiritual leaders who expressed this attitude by saying, 'I am the least of the apostles; the least of all God's people' (1 Corinthians 15.9; Ephesians 3.8).

The axis of leadership–discipleship

A disciple is a growing leader and a leader is a lifelong disciple. The same person can travel on this continuum, back and forth. This understanding of leadership and discipleship leads us to three important statements:

1 There is no leader who has never been a disciple.

2 A leader is a disciple for life.

3 Each of us functions in between leadership and discipleship all the time.

If we take Jesus as an example of the greatest of leaders, we see him throughout his earthly life as both leader and disciple. He called his disciples and led his disciples; he taught them; he influenced them; he was involved with the world. On the other hand, he listened, he prayed and sought his Father's will. His thinking was always as both leader and disciple. He saw his disciples and believers as those given by the Father (John 17), and even when he sent his disciples on mission he said that he sent them just as the Father sent him (John 20.21). So while he influenced the disciples, he also listened to the Father.

Another example was Paul. He was a great leader but also a lifelong disciple. He invited his listeners to imitate him just as he imitated Jesus Christ (1 Corinthians 11.1). Here we see Paul both lead and follow. His readers and Christ are on either side of this leadership–discipleship axis. If we go back to Figure 3.1, Paul was in position 'y' in respect of other believers, but 'x' in regard to Christ. Paul also advised Timothy to teach what he instructed him (1 Timothy 1.18). Thus Timothy became a leader at position 'y' in relation to others, but 'x' in relation to Paul.

The understanding of this principle of simultaneous leadership–discipleship is crucial in the life of all leaders. It makes them understand their status. Paul understood that he was a leader, an influencer. He reminded those who had been under him that he had done his job to the fullest extent that he knew how (Acts 20.13ff.). But at the same time he was a servant of Christ. He knew who called him. He knew he had a mission and a goal in life (1 Timothy 1.12). He understood his responsibility and to whom he was accountable at the end. This same principle also enables a person to know his stages of the leadership journey. He understands where he stands now. Paul understood this (1 Timothy 1.13–17) and he confessed in his Epistle to the church at Philippi that he had not arrived but he knew his goal and his destiny (Philippians 3.12–14).

Throughout the practice of this understanding of leadership, the faith of the person matters. Why? – Because people who are disciples of ruthless leaders will become ruthless themselves. If they are disciples of a loving person, they will love those they lead. Therefore, in reality, one becomes a disciple of the principles a leader lives. Leaders reflect the principles they believe in and the faith by which they live. Thus for a person to lead with a Christ-like character, he must know the Lord Jesus and imbibe all the principles associated with this relationship.

How are you a disciple? Which leaders or leadership principles do you follow?

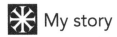 My story

Leadership

For most of my adult life I have taken leadership positions. I served as head of my class in the university, I was a teacher in school and college, an officer in a bank; a missionary to Africa, the principal of a Bible college and the principal of a seminary. I am now directing a global ministry. While holding all these positions, I had some authority invested by those who appointed me. Am I a leader because of the positions and authority I had? To a certain extent, I can say 'yes'. I had position and power. I gave supervision to those under me. I influenced many because of my positions during those various times.

Was I a leader in the eyes of the people around me? Am I a leader to them now? I think that as I held all these positions and authority, I made some lasting impact on people – my superiors, subordinates, colleagues, students and acquaintances – because of who I am and the character I exhibited.

Maybe not on all those I have dealt with, but at least on some. Perhaps there have been students along the way who were inspired and whose lives changed because of my life and my work. If so, I have been a leader with long-lasting influence on some people.

I was a youth leader in my church during the mid-1970s. Many young people looked up to me. During the late 1970s, while in the seminary in central India, God impressed upon me to write to a young lady who was one of the youth group members, to encourage her. I knew no reason why I should but I obeyed. Many months later, she told me that the letter from me came just when she was about to give up hope in her walk of faith. The letter strengthened her. The obedience to the Lord on my part bridged more than a thousand miles to encourage her and put her on the road to strong faith in the Lord. Now she and her husband serve the Lord in America. For her, my influence made a difference and so I am a leader in her eyes. Ultimately, leadership is influence.

Discipleship

How did I reach the point where I could influence people? By learning from people around me in different circumstances. In other words, I am a leader now because I was a disciple to so many people in different settings. Since one never stops learning, one is a disciple for life even while being a leader. I want to thank God for those from whom I have learned even as I continue to learn from others. And the kind of leader I am? It began the day I committed my life to Jesus. This is really the key to Christ-like leadership. This commitment changed the course of my life and my destiny. This relationship defines the kind of leadership I yearn to conduct. Paul described it well when he said,

> I have been crucified with Christ and I no longer live, but Christ lives in me. The life I live in the body, I live by faith in the Son of God, who loved me and gave himself for me.   (Galatians 2.20)

I grew up in a poor family. My parents could not afford to send me to school but my maternal uncle and aunt supported me until I completed university. But I learned from every one of them. My parents were people of faith and people of prayer. When I was small, I saw their prayerful example. So they left a legacy for me as I learned to understand the power of prayer. From my maternal uncle and aunt, I learned the importance of relationships and the power of generosity. My uncle passed away recently to be with the Lord. For me he will always be one of those who shaped me in my journey.

I grew up in a devoted and dedicated family. I knew what the local church was and what it meant. But I also knew that growing up in the Church and in a dedicated family is not enough. One needs to have a personal experience with the Lord. I learned this from my pastors and my church doctrines.

Before I finished high school I saw my sinfulness and accepted Christ as my personal Saviour, and life was never the same again.

Just before I completed university in 1973, I heard God's call to the ministry. Growing up poor I fought it for three years. I knew that one cannot be in the ministry and be rich. But while I struggled with God's call, there was a man of God who encouraged me to respond positively. I became his disciple and learned from him. Perhaps this is the reason why I want my life to be an encouragement to others. I want to continue learning how to encourage others.

While I was in the seminary in 1977, I was diagnosed with tuberculosis. As I started the treatment, I was isolated from other students for some time. My room-mate was asked to leave our room. He refused and the seminary relented, allowing him to stay with me. His decision meant more than all the medicines in the world. Thirty years later, I still feel the power of the empathy from that brother. It has made me a leader who wants to feel and empathize with the suffering and the rejected.

When God called me to the ministry, I had a problem. My family was still poor then and could not fund me to go to the seminary. I was supported through the help of Dr I. Ben Wati, a man of God well known in India and who now lives in England. I became his disciple. In other words, I learned many things from him. Once he told a story that affected me very deeply. He narrated that while he was in Shillong as a student he prayed that he might be like a pine tree. Shillong is surrounded by pines. A pine tree is always tall and straight, and because of its needle leaves birds do not normally nest in it. Dr Wati wanted to be a person of integrity, straight and open like a pine tree. I learned this from him and continue to live by this principle of integrity, and want to lead accordingly.

There have been many times when I have had to unlearn things. I have had to repent and change in order for me to become a better leader or influencer. Recently, I asked my three boys what were some of the things their mum and I did wrong as we brought them up. They were very candid. We realized there were things that we should have done that we did not do, and things we did that we should not have done. In that scenario, humility calls for repentance and asking for forgiveness. Even though we knew they had forgiven us for our failings, we asked them formally to forgive us. In their replies to our questions, we were very encouraged that there were many things they would like to repeat when they are parents. Thus we are leaders for them. Even our failings influenced them because they realize that they should not repeat those with their own families.

There are many other discipleship–leadership circumstances that I learned from. The important question is, where do I want to go from here? I want to keep influencing people, meaning that I want to continue to be a leader. It does not matter where I go, what I do and in what area of life; my desire is to influence, and thus further God's kingdom. I want to influence someone so that a person may become a better leader and influence someone else. I want to influence situations so that people will have a better environment in which to live. I want to influence institutions so that they will fulfil the purposes for which they were called into existence.

With this desire to keep on leading I also know that I need to keep on learning. Discipleship is a lifelong pursuit for me. I have some people to whom I look up. Some are my supervisors; some are my subordinates; some are family members; some are my students; some are friends; some are my neighbours; some are my acquaintances and some are even strangers. I want to keep listening to powerful preachers and teachers. I read books regularly and learn principles of leadership. My faith is important and the Bible becomes a daily guide for the kind of leader I want to be. I know very well that in the journey of discipleship I will never graduate because there are so many things to learn.

Are you a team leader? If so, in what areas are *you* are learning right now to make you a good leader?

 Biblical teaching

The Bible is full of examples of the importance of leadership and learning, both in attitude and practice. We have seen the examples of Jesus and Paul but I would like to look at a few more people from the pages of both testaments. These figures, I believe, represent the importance of learning in order to lead. Take time to read through these stories yourself and discover examples of leadership in obedience to God.

Old Testament

Moses and his call (Exodus 1—4)

We know the story well. Moses was a Hebrew child born during the time when Pharaoh wanted to kill all the Hebrew male children. The ingenuity and courage of Moses' mother facilitated the adoption of Moses as a son of Pharaoh's daughter. He became a great leader but without God's character. Moses had to run away when he killed an Egyptian. God called him when he had nothing. Even the sheep he was taking care of did not belong to him but to his father-in-law. When he responded to God, he was willing to start at the bottom – unlearning all the things that are ungodly and learning anew by depending on others, such as his brother Aaron and his father-in-law, Jethro. Through the process of lifelong discipleship, Moses became the great leader who led Israel out of slavery.

Moses and Joshua

Moses led the people of Israel through the wilderness. Before he could take them to the Promised Land he was told that he could not go but instead should anoint Joshua to take them. Even at an advanced age of more than

100 years, he had to learn obedience and humility. So he entrusted to Joshua the leadership by saying, 'Be strong and courageous . . . the LORD himself goes before you' (Deuteronomy 31.7–8). Joshua saw Moses' example and, on taking over, followed his principle of leadership. During the time that the Israelites fought the Philistines, Joshua said to his army commanders, 'Do not be afraid; do not be discouraged. Be strong and courageous. This is what the LORD will do to all the enemies you are going to fight' (Joshua 10.25). Just as Moses remained true to God till the end, Joshua did too, and said this to all the people of his day, 'But as for me and my household, we will serve the LORD' (Joshua 24.15).

Elijah and Elisha (2 Kings 2)

Elisha was the disciple of Elijah. There seemed to be a strong desire on the part of Elisha to inherit the leadership style and power of Elijah. He had lived with him, learned from him and wanted to be a prophet greater than him. I doubt it was an ego trip but I assume it was a desire to serve as Elijah did. So Elisha asked for a double portion of Elijah's power and he got it. Here was a disciple who had a clear goal of leadership, who had the tenacity to pursue it, and in humility took the challenge when it was presented to him.

New Testament

The call of Jesus to the 12 disciples (Matthew 4.18–22; Mark 3.13–19)

When Jesus called the 12 to be his disciples, he invited them to follow him. When they accepted the invitation, their goal and purpose in life changed. They learned from Jesus, the master and leader. They had to unlearn many things and learn new things. Jesus influenced them to the extent that, even when he was gone, they continued to live the way he taught them. Throughout their lives they continued learning even when Jesus had returned to the Father. A clear example was Peter, who betrayed Jesus. After Jesus was crucified, Peter went fishing again. Jesus came and met him at the lakeside and Peter learned anew the meaning of love and commitment (John 21.15ff.). Later Peter learned about the mission to the Gentiles as God prepared him for his encounter with Cornelius (Acts 10).

The book of Acts

The whole book of Acts is an example of discipleship learned. In chapter 8, we see the persecution of the Church when believers were scattered everywhere. Stephen had just been martyred. One would think that the believers would be afraid. But the Bible tells us that they shared what they had learned with everyone they met and wherever they went, and the Church grew. In other words, the discipleship principles that they had learned turned them into great leaders and influencers.

Peter the elder to his fellow elders and young men (1 Peter 5)

After Jesus gave Peter a second chance he continued as leader of the early Church, encouraging and teaching others to lead by example. He called young men to a life of discipleship, knowing that some day they would become elders themselves. He called everyone to a life of humility because this is a vital characteristic that God uses to lift people up as great leaders.

Paul, a disciple till the end

In spite of the fact that Paul influenced so many people as a leader he was a disciple throughout. There were things that he needed to learn and unlearn. He wrote to the church in Rome about the struggle he had with sin. But he praised God for the victory in Jesus Christ (Romans 7) Earlier on as a missionary he parted company with Barnabas because he did not like John Mark's behaviour (Acts 15.36–41). But later on he called John Mark his beloved son who was profitable for the ministry (1 Peter 5.13; 2 Timothy 4.11). It clearly shows what Paul learned along the way. By his own admission in his Epistle to the Philippians, he said that he had not achieved the goal of being Christ-like but that he was moving towards it (Philippians 3.14). It was only towards the end of his life that he could write,

> I have fought the good fight, I have finished the race, I have kept the faith. Now there is in store for me the crown of righteousness, which the Lord, the righteous Judge, will award to me on that day – and not only to me, but also to all who have longed for his appearing. (2 Timothy 4.7–8).

Paul died about AD 67. Through the span of time, Paul as a disciple kept unlearning and relearning many things. Hence he became a great leader.

As we close this section, we see that discipleship is a lifelong task. Moses learned every step of the way till the very end. All the 12 disciples except Judas remained faithful until the end, and as they travelled to that end they kept learning because they kept failing. Paul kept learning till the end. And so must each one who aspires to be an effective leader. That is true discipleship.

What does the Bible teach us about leadership and discipleship?

 # Effective leadership

Be a disciple

Discipleship is more difficult than leadership. It calls all the time for learning and changing. It calls all the time for unlearning, learning, relearning and changing. The more people are open to discipleship, the more effective leaders they will become. It is important that they develop an enduring spirit, being willing to learn from and listen to other leaders. They must be willing and courageous enough to change their lives and live with an eternal perspective.

But this is not easy. To be a true disciple and a true learner, one has to overcome the self – the self of pride and selfishness. Leading the self is the most difficult part. We need to ask ourselves a question: what do we do with the self? We need to guard our heart as the book of Proverbs reminds us (4.23). Our heart is the wellspring of life. When self is on the throne of our heart, bad things will come out. The way to dethrone the self is only by the power of the Holy Spirit.

Know who you are and your abilities

People lead best in those areas in which they are gifted. Each person comes to this world with gifts or abilities. They are God-given and he gives them to a person for a purpose. We know God is the Creator and he created each of us in a unique way, blessed with abilities to fulfil our roles in the world, and he does it with perfection. Whatever God calls us to do, he has already provided us with the ability to do. People who know their abilities know their limitations too. I found this out the hard way. When I was small I loved music. I bought a guitar and books on how to play the guitar, and I practised again and again. But I never learned to play because I had no gift or ability. I wasted time and money. I would never lead or influence anyone in music. Since then, I have learned to concentrate more on those abilities with which I am endowed.

Be willing to start from the bottom

Some people want to start from a position of influence. It does not work that way. One must be willing to start from the bottom, from a position of weakness and humility. Remember Jesus' parable of the talents and be ready to begin with whatever you have. Do not be like the man who had one talent and refused to use it. Use everything you have been given. Jesus started life in a manger. For 30 years he led a normal life until one day he began teaching and healing the sick. The rest is history. If you want to make history, then be willing to start from the lowest point.

Be open to everyone and everything around you

To be a leader, you must open yourself to the world of people, things, circumstances and change happening around you. You must open your mind, your heart and your life to others. Those around you must also see this openness in order to enable them to share your growth. Ask yourself, are you set in your ways? Do you feel that there is no more to learn or no more room for growth? Whenever we think we have arrived, that is the end of our growth in leadership. This needs to change. This attitude needs to be broken. We must commit to dealing with the old that is no longer working and learn new things. Only when this 'brokenness' occurs will we be opened to growth.

Choose your mentors

People who want to be effective leaders must realize that there are people who know more than they do. They should understand that there are people from whom they can learn and who can provide counsel. Thus people can make choices about whom they seek help from. Besides putting themselves under the Holy Spirit, such people need mentors and principles with which to work.

Keep learning

There is one constant in the world, and that is change. The world is changing at lightning speed. Knowledge dates quickly. Skills that are useful today will not be tomorrow. With knowledge and usable skills ever changing, those in leadership ought to constantly update themselves if they want to remain effective. Any leaders who refuse to relearn even things they are already familiar with will be left behind and become irrelevant.

Learn from different sources

The resources that leaders can learn from are limitless. If a person wants to grow in Christ-like leadership, God through his Holy Spirit and through his word are the sources of all wisdom. But other sources are the people around us; the media (audio, visual and printed); events of different kinds; experiences of all sorts (good and bad, pleasant and sad); and we can even learn from nature. We learn through observation, through meditation, by listening, by reading, through interacting and by doing.

Put into action what you have learned

'Practice makes perfect' goes the saying. Leaders must always put into practice what they are learning so that they can grow. There are those who learned and learned but never put that learning into practice. Such people will have swelled heads but shrivelled hearts and withered hands. They cannot be called leaders in the truest sense of the word, for they will influence no one. Putting learning into practice not only helps those doing it; it also helps them to help others. A leader who has been mentored needs to mentor others.

Connect with others

No one can live in an isolated world. A person who is not willing to connect with others cannot help, lead or influence others. Connection is a risk because you build a relationship. You get to know people and they get to know you. Through connection you learn to understand people and empathize with them. In relationship you learn to work together. There is power in team work and networking. A person multiplies himself many times when he or she is connected with others. Networking is a powerful platform for learning and leading. And everyone who wants to be a leader needs to be positive about it.

1 All great leaders have one thing in common: they connect with people.

2 Connecting with people is the leader's responsibility.

3 Connection starts with the heart. One connects only when one feels.

4 Connection requires positive effort.

Depend totally on God

There is a popular saying: 'Do everything as if it depends on you but pray as if everything depends on God.' One cannot begin to be a disciple without the initiation of God and one cannot grow towards leadership without the help of God. In prayer we connect with God, asking for his constant help. Leaders throughout Scripture and history turned out to be great because of their dependence on prayer. We can think of many examples of prayer for various needs and in many circumstances. Each prayer made the person a better leader.

Abraham prayed and God healed (Genesis 20.17). Moses prayed when people sinned and God heard him, strengthening his leadership (Numbers 21.7ff.). Elisha prayed and the Lord opened the eyes of his young servant to see the power of God (2 Kings 6.17). King Hezekiah prayed and he was given a new lease of life that lasted for 15 years (2 Kings 20.1–21). Jonah prayed and he got out of trouble (Jonah 2.1). Daniel prayed and God helped him to remain faithful in a foreign land (Daniel 6.10ff.). The disciples of Jesus prayed to get a new leader to replace Judas Iscariot (Acts 1.24–26). Peter prayed for Tabitha who was dead and she sat up alive (Acts 9.40). A midnight prayer made the prison bars crumble for Paul and Silas (Acts 16.25ff.). Paul prayed and healed a secular person (Acts 28.8). What a testimony! The best example of prayer though is from our Lord Jesus. He made it a habit to pray and often withdrew himself to a solitary place (Luke 5.16). He prayed for his disciples as a group and for individual needs (Luke 22.32). And he prayed for strength when he had to go through Gethsemane (Luke 22.41–44).

It is in prayer that disciples turned into great influencers as the Holy Spirit filled them, shook them, changed them and sent them in boldness (Acts 4.31). Remember that a fervent prayer of a person in the right relationship with God prevails (James 5.16). May you be a leader who is a disciple of prayer.

Which title would you rather choose?

Would you choose to be called a disciple or a leader? For a Christ-like leader, a discipleship attitude helps you to understand that you constantly learn from the Lord Jesus. It makes you realize that there is no destination this side of heaven but a constant learning. You continue to learn not only from Jesus but from life, for there are new avenues to conquer; new mountains to climb, new depths to ponder, new people to become acquainted with and influence. On the other hand, a disciple of Jesus Christ has no choice but to be a leader or an influencer in Jesus' name. Leadership is a by-product of discipleship. Whatever a disciple does, however a disciple speaks and acts, he or she influences others, and very often those who are influenced call the disciple a leader. Anyone, therefore, who wants to be a leader must prepare for a lifetime of discipleship.

 QUESTIONS

1 What are the areas in which you lead best? Compare these with your abilities. Learn to concentrate on those, rather than on the ones for which you have no gift.

2 Are you a leader on a team, or teams, right now? Think of those areas in which you can contribute to your team.

3 What are the areas in which you are lacking, and where you know others can contribute?

4

Leadership and prophetic ministry

Sue Fenton

 Introduction

Can you imagine what it must be like to be given the gift of hearing in your mid-forties after being deaf since birth? This has recently been the case for a friend of mine. She is married and has two young children, and has been deaf all her life. Earlier this year she underwent a cochlear implant procedure, which can provide hearing sensations for some severely and profoundly deaf individuals who derive no benefit from hearing aids.

This woman is hearing for the first time in her life. The challenge for her now is to make sense of what she is hearing. Her constant question seems to be, 'What's that sound?' It is a challenge for her to interpret the meaning of things we take for granted, such as the sound of a washing machine going through its cycle, people laughing, wind in the trees, a telephone ringing or a dog barking. Hence, although this is a miraculous procedure, a great deal of personal commitment is required for this woman to make headway regarding *how to listen* and, more importantly, *how to make sense of what she is now hearing*. In order for her to learn to speak clearly, many months of speech therapy are required, as the ability to hear and speak are closely intertwined. This interlinking of hearing and speaking, as we shall see, is at the heart of prophetic leadership.

By the time we reach chapter 50 of the book of Isaiah, the people of Israel had been held in exile by the Babylonians for many years, and were probably giving up hope of ever being able to return to Jerusalem. Words from the prophet of hope and encouragement, and of God's promise to 'save' them, were most likely met with scorn and cynicism. They were tired and losing their energy to maintain faith and hope in their state of captivity. Isaiah 50.4–9 begins with the prophet stating that God has given him the tongue of a teacher *so that* he may sustain these weary ones with a word of hope.

As people in ministry leadership, or training for ministry leadership, a large part of our role is to speak hope, but not just with words. What an awesome responsibility and privilege it is to think that God might have given us ears to hear and tongues to sustain weary people!

> Who are the weary in your community and church? What does this weariness look like in today's world?

In order to speak clearly, it is imperative that we can hear. In this passage from Isaiah it is God who enables the prophet to hear. What a picture of utter dependence on God for this calling to prophetic ministry: 'He wakens me morning by morning, wakens my ear . . . The Sovereign LORD has opened my ear' (Isaiah 50.4–5).

God also gave the prophets tongues to challenge the religious activities and focus of his people, as they had become immersed in their sanctuary-bound piety and worship, and deaf to the sounds of the poor and oppressed. The prophet was called to challenge the self-centred preoccupations of the people of God and to remind them of the true focus of worship.

> What words of hope and encouragement do you offer when they are needed?

More often than not in the Scriptures, the prophet's message challenged the religious people of the day, rather than the community. It is easy to view the main role of the prophet today as being to challenge unjust governments and corrupt leaders who oppress certain groups and so perpetuate poverty and discrimination. Yet it is just as important that the prophetic voice is heard inside the Church.

We who profess to follow the greatest prophet of all time, Jesus Christ, Son of God, are often so busy attending to maintaining church life that we fail to see injustice, abuse and oppression in the Church. For years, abuse of children has been covered up in many churches and allowed to continue, while at the same time in these churches sermons are being preached from the pulpit on our sinfulness and God's love, grace and forgiveness.

In this chapter I will explore various aspects of leadership and prophetic ministry by looking first at a case study concerning domestic violence and child abuse from my own context in New Zealand. I will then reflect on prophetic leadership from a biblical and theological viewpoint, looking particularly at several passages from Isaiah and Amos in the Old Testament, Jesus' prophetic ministry, and women prophets. Lastly, I will look briefly at renewal movements in church history, focusing on the Reformed tradition, and some contemporary examples of prophetic ministry initiatives from the UK, Australia and New Zealand.

Whatever country we live in, we ought not to be deaf to the strident sounds of global issues such as hunger, poverty, war and racism, violence, HIV & AIDS, injustice, oppression and exploitation, especially of women and children. Each of us will be aware of areas of concern in our own countries and local communities, where the good news of the gospel needs to be spoken, and prophetic communities of faith need to demonstrate an alternative to the status quo. As the Church we need to be asking questions in our own situations.

Where are the dark places in our societies today in which we as the people of God can be light? How can we be Christ in our communities? How can we exercise prophetic ministry in situations of oppression and weariness?

A case study from New Zealand

A distressing and appalling sound coming from homes across my country of New Zealand today is that of domestic violence, especially towards women and children. Some recently released figures from the Organization for Economic Co-operation and Development do not present a positive picture of New Zealand society, especially for a country that used to be known for its high standard of living and innovative welfare system. In health and safety, New Zealand ranks twenty-third out of 24 OECD countries, and it is rated the third highest for child homicide through maltreatment. In 2006, 16,738 women and 12,701 children used refuges run by the National Collective of Women (and this does not include refuges run by other organizations). In 2006 there were 63,000 recorded incidents of family violence involving more than 200,000 people. This is in a country of only four million people. Although these figures are worrying, it is not until we hear the individuals' stories making up these statistics that the real horror of the situation penetrates our consciousness.

Nia Glasse, a three-year-old girl from Rotorua in the North Island of New Zealand, died on 3 August 2007 after being subjected to horrific abuse, including being put in a clothes dryer and hung on a washing line. Five people, including her stepfather, have been charged with assault.

On 23 July 2000, a 23-month-old baby girl called Lillybing died from dreadful injuries inflicted by abuse. She had been left in the care of her step-aunt, as her own mother, a 28-year-old, was pregnant with her fifth child and not coping. Lillybing had been falling over and was hard to wake. A friend of the family who had been babysitting her urged the family to rush her to hospital. Upon arriving at the hospital, it was discovered that the baby girl had been dead for between five and seven hours and had sustained a massive facial burn, injuries to the vagina and stomach, and a fatal brain haemorrhage. She had been beaten about the legs in an attempt to toilet-train her, burnt with a cloth soaked in boiling water applied to a lump on her head, and shaken so violently when she was crying that she suffered a brain haemorrhage. The evidence relating to the vaginal injuries remains unresolved.

A recent headline in our daily newspaper read, 'Five-year-old high on P in drug house'. The police had found a five-year-old boy high on P, or methamphetamine, during a raid on a drug house. The police officer said,

'He was swearing and literally climbing the walls . . . I've never seen a child behave like that before.' In 2007, 90 children were known to have been exposed to the manufacture of P in their homes. These children were removed from their parents by social workers who had to dress in decontamination suits, have a special bath and be given a blood test for toxins. The children were then placed in foster care.

These stories are only the tip of the iceberg. Yet many of the churches in New Zealand are strangely inactive on this issue. Prayers may be said during a time of intercession in a Sunday morning service, but is this enough? Of course there are individual Christians whose work involves them in the day-to-day realities of these situations, as doctors, aid-agency workers and foster-carers, but how much of the Church's financial resources, human resources, time and energy go into addressing this and other horrendous issues of injustice in our society? How many leaders and staff working in churches are spending paid time trying to connect with these families? Have our carefully crafted worship services, high-quality preaching, inspiring contemporary music and appealing children's programmes deafened us to the sounds in the homes next door to our church buildings?

> Can our worship sometimes prevent us from seeing injustice in our communities? How do we relate Christian worship and prayer to working for justice?

This is precisely the kind of problem the prophets were called to address. Isaiah 58, which will be discussed at greater length later, talks of the worshippers' frustration at trying to draw near to God through fasting, prayer, worship and humbling themselves, but still sensing that God is far away and not listening. God's reply, in contemporary terms, is along these lines:

> If you start caring about injustice, child abuse, violence, hunger and poverty, beaten women and drunken teenagers, then you will know the glory of the Lord, and I will answer your prayers. You will be the light of the world, and I will guide you and give you strength.

Biblical and theological reflection

Prophetic ministry in the Old Testament

A large proportion of our canon, particularly the Old Testament, has prophetic content. Apart from the major and minor prophetic books, prophecy, as re-imagining reality, is a recurring theme in the Torah, Psalms and Wisdom literature. In the book of Exodus, Moses dismantled the religion of static triumphalism and replaced it with an alternative religion of the freedom of God. He countered the politics of oppression and exploitation by countering it with the politics of justice and compassion.

The prophets of the Old Testament and Jesus, Paul and others in the New Testament were called to speak God's word of truth to the people. This was often a difficult and unwelcome calling, and frequently fraught with danger. It was at times a message of truth in the face of denial – hard words to hear – but they also spoke hope to despair. In many cases their message came because the people of God had lost sight of what God had called them to be, as his representatives in the world. When the religious rituals and Temple worship lost touch with the needs of the poor, the marginalized and oppressed, and ignored injustice and the need for compassion, the prophets were called to remind the people about God's vision of how society should function according to kingdom principles, and their role in this as God's people.

Prophecy is so much more than 'foretelling the future'. According to Walter Brueggemann's definition, prophecy is a re-imagining or re-speaking of society and the Church in accordance with God's word. In more contemporary language, prophets and apostles could be described as questioners and protesters, often visionaries and sometimes the initiators of new ventures. Brueggemann, in his book *The Prophetic Imagination*, has said,

> The time may be ripe in the church for serious consideration of prophecy as a crucial element in ministry . . . prophets understood the distinctive power of language, the capacity to speak in ways that evoke newness 'fresh from the Word'. (Brueggemann, 2001, p. xxiii)

Prophets were outside the established authority of the day. They had an acute capacity to practise social analysis, but not necessarily social action. They seemed to be able to combine a sense of holiness that is needed to sustain society with a holistic understanding of how social reality functions. They often displayed an intimate spiritual life rooted in the reality of God, and dared to imagine that God is the hope of the world.

Prophets were characteristically poets, who worked with symbols, metaphors and words, which enabled them to get underneath assumed public reality and to subvert this reality. Brueggemann makes the point that the Church today often sees prophets as simply denouncers and critics, but this is not the case. The task of a prophet is to bring truth to denial, and hope to despair. Lament, rather than anger, is a key part of the prophetic process. In order for the prophetic ministry to return to the Church, we need to return to the rhetoric of the text, and let the text shape our utterance and imagination. It will be the text that enables the Church to engage in a subversive imagination of a world functioning according to the gospel and the kingdom of God.

It is clearly impossible to do justice to all the biblical prophetic writings in a chapter of this length, so I have chosen to focus, as a case study, on the theme of hope in a state of exile in the book of Isaiah generally, and Isaiah 58 in particular, and on some themes from Amos, in order to provide some concrete examples of how the prophetic text may inform our thinking in the Church today.

Hope is interwoven through the entire book of Isaiah as a golden thread winds through a tapestry. Isaiah is essentially a prophetic portrayal of the history of Jerusalem between approximately 740 and 520 BC. The pivot point of the book is between chapters 39 and 40. The gap between these two chapters encompasses two centuries from when Jerusalem was destroyed by the Babylonians in 587 BC to the people's return from exile. According to Brueggemann in *An Introduction to the Old Testament* (2003, p. 159), 'The book of Isaiah . . . is a meditation . . . about the destiny of Jerusalem into the crises of exile and the promise of Jerusalem out of exile into new well-being.'

Hope is about expecting and imagining something to happen. It is about the future rather than the present. Hope is about recognizing and embracing the darkness, and recognizing that there is one who can be trusted with this darkness and is more powerful than those who appear to rule the light. It is energizing, freeing and motivating, and refuses to accept the current reality as the reality that God intended.

Isaiah 58.1–10 begins with a clear command from God to the prophet, to shout out and not to hold back. There is a sense of stridency and boldness in the rhetoric. It is the house of Jacob that is being addressed, the people, the community; and the topic is their rebellion and sin. Surprisingly, verse 2 proceeds to describe the people's seeming devotion to God: day after day they seek God, and they want to know God's ways. They seem to be a people wanting to follow God, and they delight in drawing near to God. Verse 3 then goes on to express the questions of the people to God. They are saying, 'Why are you silent, God? We are carrying out all the correct religious practices, but you still seem far away.' God replies that although the people appear to be saying all the right words, their actions and deeds to others are not pleasing to God. As Kwesi Dickson comments in an article in the *International Review of Mission*,

> Evidently a great deal of emphasis had come to be placed on this aspect of religion – speaking out and seeking answers. In their preoccupation they had failed to realize that speaking to God, essential as that was, was not the only component of religion; our prophets show that doing is another, and complementary component. (Dickson, 1977, p. 230)

Verse 6 goes on to describe the kind of fasting or worship God requires, and instead of being directed towards God, the fasting recommended by the prophet seems to be directed toward human beings. The authenticity of the people's religious devotion was questionable due to their lack of social concern, and the rituals associated with worship had become wooden. The sacred and the secular had become separated and unrelated to each other. There should be no distinction between worshipping God and serving one's fellow human beings. Worship and life are inseparable.

Verses 8 to 10 express the hope and promises of God: 'Then your light will break forth like the dawn, and your healing will quickly appear.' The imagery of light breaking into darkness is a powerful one, and implies totally changed circumstances. As Dickson has noted, 'One comes out of the gloom of unsatisfying religious pursuit to the glory of being truly in the presence of God' (1977, p. 230).

In conclusion, hope is threaded through the entire tapestry of Isaiah but particularly in this passage. The following poem, which I wrote myself, expresses the theme of hope as found in Isaiah.

Hope – a gift freely spoken
redescribing the world
light instead of darkness
freedom, joy, release
    do not fear, do not fear

God cries out
I am your redeemer, come home with me

    nourishment instead of thirst and hunger
    fruitfulness instead of barrenness
    singing instead of mourning

a new kingdom
a new reign
waiting and trusting
energy, identity
righteousness, justice, peace
steadfast love, healing, restoration
pardon
forgiveness
hope, a gift.

Frederick Holmgren, in *Priests and Prophets: Spirituality and Social Conscience* (2005), focuses his examination on the book of Amos. He notes how the worshippers who were gathered at the holy sanctuaries of Bethel and Gilgal would have been angered and shocked by the divine anger spoken through Amos with regard to their worship. He points out how 'the worship at these holy places is marked by a sanctuary-bound piety that ignores elemental acts of justice and kindness on the street' (p. 304).

God's ear is turned towards only those worshippers who want 'justice to roll on like a river, righteousness like a never-failing stream' (Amos 5.24). Amos is not calling for a religion without a place for corporate worship, but rather pointing out that worship needs to be accompanied by obedience to God's other commands to seek justice and compassion for the poor and powerless. Worship and social action need to be woven closely together, for either element on its own becomes powerless and hollow. Communities of faith need the prophet, but the prophet also needs the community of faith.

Can you think of an individual or group in your community that are already practising a prophetic ministry? (They may or may not be part of an established church.)

Prophetic ministry in the New Testament

There are many interpretations and views in New Testament studies on what constitutes a prophet. One definition states, 'The prophesying of the New Testament prophets was both the preaching of the Divine counsels of grace already accomplished and the foretelling of the purposes of God in the future' (Vine et al., 1985, p. 904). The word 'prophet' occurs many times in the Gospels, and in Paul's Epistles to various churches. The apostle Paul placed apostles and prophets in first and second place in two of his lists of gifts (1 Corinthians 12.28–31; Ephesians 4.11), and included prophecy in the other two lists (Romans 12.6–8; 1 Corinthians 12.8–10).

Jesus was often perceived by the crowds as a prophet (Matthew 21.11, 46; Luke 7.16), especially after he had performed a miracle. All four Gospels make the point that Jesus was rejected in Nazareth because a prophet is not honoured in his hometown (Matthew 13.57; Mark 6.4; Luke 4.24; John 4.44). Jesus himself lamented that the prophets that had been sent to Jerusalem in the past had been rejected, killed or flogged (Matthew 23.37), and he knew he was destined for the same fate.

Jesus demonstrated the prophetic ministry of lament and criticism, but also of energizing and amazement. As Brueggemann states,

> Clearly Jesus cannot be understood simply as a prophet, for that designation, like every other, is inadequate for the historical reality of Jesus. Nonetheless, among his other functions it is clear that Jesus functioned as a prophet. In both his teaching and his very presence, Jesus of Nazareth presented the ultimate criticism of the royal consciousness. (Brueggemann, 2001, p. 82)

The way in which Jesus provided this criticism was through his solidarity with people who were on the margins of 'acceptable' society. This was demonstrated initially by his birth, and the radical inversion that was embodied in it (Luke 1.51–53). This radicalism continued throughout his life, especially with regard to his announcement of the kingdom in both words and actions. He forgave people far too readily, he broke the Sabbath by healing the sick, he had table fellowship with outcasts, and upset the moral order of the day by showing grace to those who did not deserve it.

Jesus showed compassion to those who were hurting, which challenged the numbness of his social context and of the empire. He noticed and identified with pain and suffering. He included people such as women and children, and in so doing showed a scandalous breach of decorum. His critique concerned the fundamental social valuing of his society. His words and actions were prophetic and profound, but severely threatening to those who were in power.

Intertwined with Jesus' criticism and pathos were energizing acts and amazement. He not only dismantled the dominant world-view but also offered a new beginning in the form of the kingdom of God, and the freedom, justice and compassion this kingdom offers. People who embraced Jesus' ministry were transformed when they encountered him. Luke 7.22 says that through this encounter the blind receive sight, the lame walk, lepers are cleansed, the deaf hear, the dead are raised up, and the poor receive good news.

According to Brueggemann, the resurrection is the ultimate act of prophetic energizing. He comments,

> The resurrection can only be received and affirmed and celebrated as the new action of God whose province it is to create new futures for people and to let them be amazed in the midst of despair . . .
> It is a new history open to all but peculiarly received by the marginal victims of the old order. The fully energized Lord of the church is not some godly figure in the sky but the slain Lamb who stood outside the royal domain and was punished for it. (Brueggemann, 2001, pp. 112–13)

A biblical foundation for women prophets

In both the Old and New Testaments, female as well as male prophets are mentioned. As Linda Belleville reminds us, 'There are numerous examples of women prophets, stretching back to Mosaic times. In fact, if there is one gift women consistently possessed and exercised throughout the history of God's people, it is this one' (Belleville, 2000, p. 55).

In the Old Testament, women prophets include Miriam, Moses' sister; Deborah; Shallum's wife Huldah; and Noadiah. Luke 2.36 speaks of a prophetess, Anna, who was the daughter of Phanuel, of the tribe of Asher. She was an elderly woman, who was married for seven years, then widowed into her old age. Luke tells us that she never left the Temple, but worshipped there with fasting and prayer night and day. She prophesied about Jesus to all those who were looking for Jerusalem to be redeemed. In Acts 21.9, it is mentioned that Philip, the evangelist, had four unmarried daughters who were all prophetesses.

Cheryl Sanders has written *Ministry at the Margins: The Prophetic Mission of Women, Youth and the Poor*. She describes the actions of the woman in Mark 14.3–9, who anointed Jesus with costly ointment, as a prophetic sign of his impending death and burial. The disciples seem to miss the symbolic significance of her action, and Sanders suggests this was because they were in denial about Jesus' impending death and resurrection. In Sanders' words,

> She had acted out of an understanding beyond their comprehension, she knew what they could not grasp, she did what they never would have thought to do . . . She demonstrated the courage and initiative of a prophet, one who is willing to speak for God (if not with words, with symbolic actions). She acted in obedience to God, even when nobody else understood or accepted what she was trying to do. (Sanders, 1997, p. 53)

Sanders warns that anyone doing ministry should expect opposition and at times to be misunderstood. She states that opposition often comes from those from whom we would expect support, and the story of this woman in Mark illustrates this point. It was the disciples, Jesus' closest followers, who criticized her actions, but it was Jesus who defended her. Jesus says in Mark 14.9 that where the good news is told, this woman's actions will be told in remembrance of her. There is clearly much to be done in recovering this woman's story, both from the text and in the context of how this is being lived out in the lives of women in prophetic ministry today. Sanders concludes,

> The woman of Bethany is a spiritual foremother to women in ministry today, and deserves to be claimed as such. Women in ministry need to take the prophetic initiative, in memory of a woman who served Christ in ways that men did not understand. Women in ministry must face all opponents, in memory of a woman who let Jesus' words become her abiding assurance and her first line of defence. (Sanders, 1997, p. 56)

In summary, prophets have been an integral part of God's mission to the world in Scripture and throughout history. They are mouthpieces that sometimes have a predictive role, but they also remind God's people of their covenant obligations, and are able to re-speak and re-imagine the world according to God's reign. In Ephesians 2.20, Paul tells the church at Ephesus that the Church is built on the foundations laid by the apostles and prophets, with Jesus as the cornerstone. Some key indicators of prophetic ministry can be an initial dissatisfaction with the way things are, then comes a God-inspired rebirth or new birth.

 ## Prophetic ministry in the Reformed tradition

Throughout church history, movements have arisen to renew the Church. Prior to the Reformation, the many monastic movements were attempts to revitalize and reform the Church, and bring it back to what was perceived to be its original purpose. The Protestant Reformation was yet another sign that the Church must continually renew itself, and John Calvin, along with Martin Luther and others, was a key figure in this movement. It is interesting that Calvin saw himself primarily as a scholar and thinker, not as a leader or pastor. Justo González in *The Story of Christianity*. Vol. 2: *The Reformation to the Present Day* has summarized Calvin's reluctant entry into a prophetic reforming role:

> Calvin arrived at Geneva in 1536 with the firm intention of stopping there for no more than a day . . . But someone told William Farel [leader of the so-called Bern missionaries] that Calvin was in town, and the result was an unforgettable interview. Farel, who 'burned with a marvellous zeal for the advancement of the gospel,' presented Calvin with several reasons why his presence was needed in

Geneva. Calvin listened respectfully . . . but refused to heed Farel's plea, telling him that he had planned certain studies . . . Farel then challenged Calvin with a dire threat: 'May God condemn your repose, and the calm you seek for study, if before such a great need you withdraw, and refuse your succor and help.' Calvin later wrote, 'these words shocked and broke me, and I desisted from the journey I had planned.' Thus began his career as the Reformer of Geneva.

(González, 1985, p. 65)

The Great Awakening (early eighteenth century) and the Second Great Awakening in the nineteenth century in America are also examples of renewal movements which changed the Church and included leaders from the Reformed tradition. This tradition was instrumental in the great Pietistic renewals sweeping Europe and North America which led to the Great Awakening. The involvement of Reformed leaders in these renewal movements has been summarized in this way:

> Presbyterians were divided by a controversy between those who insisted on strict adherence to the teachings of Westminster – the Old Side – and those of the New Side, whose emphasis was on the experience of redeeming grace . . . This led to schism – a schism made more acute due to the great Pietistic wave known as the Great Awakening . . . The first signs of the Great Awakening appeared in Northampton, Massachusetts. The pastor there was Jonathan Edwards, a staunch Calvinist who was now convinced of the need for a personal experience of conversion . . . In 1734 people began responding to his sermons . . . many with a remarkable change in their lives . . . The ministers of the New Side joined the revival . . . and extraordinary responses were evoked in their churches. (González, 1985, p. 65)

This involvement continued in the Second Great Awakening, but one telling result, described in the last sentence of the following quote (in italics), should also be noted:

> Towards the end of the 18th century, a Second Great Awakening began in New England. This was marked . . . by a sudden earnestness in Christian devotion and living . . . and moved beyond New England and the educated elite, making great headway among people of less education and fewer means . . . The Cane Ridge Revival of 1801, in Kentucky, marked a significant step forward in this movement. It was organized by a local Presbyterian pastor, who announced a great assembly or 'camp meeting' for the promotion of a deeper faith. On the appointed date, thousands gathered. The response . . . was overwhelming . . . *Yet, although the Cane Ridge gathering had been organized by a Presbyterian, that denomination did not favor the emotional response that was becoming part of the movement, and soon Presbyterians began taking action against ministers who participated in church revival events such as Cane Ridge.* (González, 1985, pp. 245–6)

This is unfortunately all too often the response of the established churches when prophetic renewal movements arise from within their ranks. With this historical reality in mind, we move now to consider several contemporary expressions of prophetic leadership and ministry.

✳ Contemporary examples of prophetic ministry

What place does prophetic ministry have in the leadership of the Church today?

Should the expectation of the Church be that an ordained leader be able to function equally effectively in all the gifts and functions mentioned in Ephesians 4.11 (apostle, prophet, evangelist, teacher and pastor)?

In relation specifically to prophetic leadership, how do leaders in the Church today, especially those in ordained ministry, speak as prophets from the edge, when they are entrenched in the institution of the Church? Are those gifted individuals who are called and then trained as teachers, preachers and pastors also able to undertake this prophetic task effectively? Or should the Church today also recognize, encourage and train its leadership with a more prophetic and apostolic gifting, so that these leaders can be free from the demands of traditional parish ministry in order to maintain a prophetic perspective? If so, how can this be done?

Are the expectations by others of those in ordained ministry unrealistic and unfair?

William Willimon has suggested that prophetic ministry after Pentecost is practised by the community rather than by an individual (Willimon, 2002, pp. 249–50). While it is true that the prophet needs the community of faith to help discern and validate the prophetic proclamation, and the community itself can be prophetic in the very way it lives, I would suggest that it is apparent that certain individuals have been called to speak and lead prophetically over the years since the outpouring of the Holy Spirit in Acts 2. Individuals such as Martin Luther King, Nelson Mandela and William Wilberforce have clearly been prophetic leaders. Perhaps many churches today are not as effective in the world as they could be because those individuals with a prophetic or apostolic gifting are stifled.

Yet, despite the devaluing of prophetic ministry in many of our mainstream churches (certainly in the West), it does persist, and new forms of prophetic ministry are continually emerging around the world. From a wide range of readings and many possible examples I have selected two contemporary case studies from my own context in New Zealand. I then ask what else the Church might do in practical terms, especially with regard to issues such as domestic violence and child abuse.

Youth for Christ New Zealand

Youth for Christ New Zealand is a para-church organization that operates as a national incorporated society and registered charity. It has been in operation since the 1940s and has run a variety of programmes for youth. In about 2004, Darryl Gardiner (YFCNZ National Director) led his team in facing some brutal facts about the organization. They recognized that there was a lack of younger leaders coming through into senior leadership, and that many of the youth who were making decisions to follow Christ at their various programmes were not continuing in their Christian walk as they reached adulthood. The existing staff members were struggling in their own faith, and the numbers of youth being contacted were decreasing.

I interviewed Darryl Gardiner and asked him where God was in this process, and he commented that, after facing these harsh realities about the organization, there was a clear and overwhelming consensus among the national leaders of YFCNZ that a 'rebirthing' was required. They sent some of their team overseas to do research, spent time praying and consulting, and had a strong feeling that radical change was necessary. Something else that confirmed this need for rebirth for him was that the people who had to make the decisions to change had the most to lose in terms of income, power and security, but were still prepared to make the hard calls.

Consequently, YFCNZ has made some major changes in its organization, and as part of this shake-up has ceased to run many of its existing programmes and has re-invented itself as a mission order. This means that they now see themselves as a group of people who choose to adopt a set of values and practices, or rules and rhythms of life, in a particular context, which for them is the youth community in New Zealand. There are various levels of involvement, with mainly volunteer staff, but with clear accountability and mentoring processes in place.

This move reflects a far more incarnational approach than in the past, and more of a team approach to leadership, rather than a hierarchal structure. There is now a team of three people leading the organization, with Darryl still involved though not in a national leadership role. This process has had its challenges and critics, but is a courageous step on a journey that attempts to follow in Jesus' footsteps in prophetic mission to the youth of New Zealand.

Darryl described to me an image of a redwood tree that can be dead for a hundred years before anyone realizes it. It still looks alive, but is actually dead on the inside, and one day suddenly falls over. When asked if the changes in YFCNZ are going to work, he says that he is 51 per cent sure that they will work and are right, but he is 99 per cent sure that if they had not made the changes, the organization would have eventually died.

Urban Vision

Urban Vision was formally birthed in 1996, although for Martin Robinson, Justin Duckworth and others involved, living in community as an expression of incarnational mission had been happening for a few years before this. This community has had strong links with Youth for Christ in Wellington, but more recently has developed into a more independent group.

Martin Robinson explained in my interview with him that they began by having an intentional community home (a community formed with a clear purpose in mind) in Wellington, where they had a number of disadvantaged people from the community living with them. For Martin and his wife, the group to which they have felt particularly drawn are Somali and Ethiopian refugees.

They did this informally for about four years, before Urban Vision was officially formed. Martin sees the medium of *living in community* as being a core message of the gospel. Initially their move was in part a reaction to the individualistic and insulating nature of the existing Church. They saw the Church as being 'centrifugal' and inward-looking, having a low priority on 'character' and a high priority on 'talents'. They felt called to pioneer in the direction of meeting the needs of people-groups that the Church was not reaching, using intentional Christian communities.

There are now six geographical community locations around the North Island, involving 42 adults and 21 children. Each location has a slightly different focus, with some reaching at-risk youth, others working with those living in council flats, and then the work with refugees. They have been in some respects on the margins of the Church. They do not view themselves as a church per se, but more as a 'mission order' with practices and covenants encouraged for their members.

The challenge for them going into the future is how to partner with the existing Church. The question they are asking is: 'What is it that God has birthed through Urban Vision that can be offered back to the Church?' They feel they have come full circle, and now desire to partner in some way with the established churches, but are not sure what this may look like. It is encouraging that there is a desire by incarnational mission movements, such as Urban Vision, to partner with the Church in some way, while at the same time being aware of not losing their freedom of being situated 'on the edge' or 'at the margins'.

What organizations or groups are acting prophetically in your context? Describe what makes them prophetic.

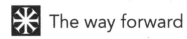 ## The way forward

In what other ways might the Church speak and act prophetically today? How can leaders who have a gift and calling in prophetic ministry be part of, but at the same time on the edge of, a faith community so as to maintain a prophetic voice? This can be a source of tension for ordained ministers, or those in paid positions in Christian leadership, as many paid roles are not focused on practising this type of ministry, but rather focused on the more traditional roles of teaching and pastoring. A 'mixed economy' approach might allow the traditional role of minister as pastor/teacher to exist alongside, and in partnership with, a role as prophet/apostle. The two roles should be regarded as complementary and necessary, rather than inappropriate and threatening. Such an approach would give a new freedom for the Church and those in ministry to connect with society in fresh ways.

The challenge to embody and practise prophetic ministry will vary according to our own contexts. One option I am exploring is to work with a charitable trust that is associated with an existing church, but sufficiently independent of it to be free to explore fresh ways of being a church and speaking prophetically in the community. This is not necessarily a comfortable or easy place to be, but prophetic ministry is not usually comfortable or easy!

In what ways could you encourage a prophetic ministry in your own context?

Listening to the sounds in the community by meeting people already working in the areas of greatest concern, and seeing what partnerships could be developed with existing agencies and the Church, is vitally important. It may be possible to speak with local political leaders about issues in the community as they see them, and find out whether there are ways for the local church to partner local community groups to address these issues. Returning to the earlier mention of domestic violence and child abuse, a prophetic ministry might entail linking Christians with at-risk families in the community, offering empathetic mentoring and family-strengthening gifts, or running parenting courses to encourage strong families.

There is a very good 12-week programme called Divorcecare, which our church has used successfully to work with adults who have experienced a broken relationship, and another one which we are wanting to start, called 'High 5', which is aimed at helping children whose parents have separated or divorced. All such programmes are ways in which the Church can speak prophetically to ways of life that have become commonplace in many societies today, and become involved in society outside the worship service on a Sunday. It is so important to show that we as the Church are not judgemental and elitist towards those who have experienced relationship breakdowns but are there to be salt and light as Jesus encouraged us to be. These are practical, small ways of addressing injustice and oppression in society, especially where children are concerned.

In March 2007 in New Zealand, the government voted and passed a piece of legislation that made the act of a parent smacking a child a criminal offence. The previous law allowed a defence lawyer to use the fact that parents were allowed to use 'reasonable force' in disciplining their children as a defence for their clients when charged with assault of their children. This resulted in many child-abuse cases being unable to be brought to a conviction.

Christians have been divided over this change in the law. Some have been strongly supportive of it, recognizing that New Zealanders' attitudes to children needed to change, and that violence under the guise of parental discipline was no longer acceptable. Others, however, doubt that the high incidence of domestic violence in New Zealand, which has resulted in many injuries and deaths of children, will be changed by the introduction of this Bill. They maintain that if parents want to use smacking as a way of disciplining their children they should be allowed to do so. These people would further argue that we should be focusing our attention on the underlying issues of parenting, drug and alcohol abuse, rather than on this type of legislation, which is helpful only after the event.

Jesus addressed the oppressive attitudes of his culture and society towards children and showed an alternative way. He allowed children to come to him, when adults would have stopped them. He made them feel accepted, loved and listened to, as one individual to another, and taught others to do the same. We would do well to begin by following his example, to value our children, and to treat them with love and respect.

In conclusion, the role of prophet is not an easy one, but a vitally necessary one for the health and accountability of the Church and society. It is important for leaders exercising prophetic ministry to remember that God desires to be the source of our hearing and speaking. It is God who is able to awaken and open our ears, morning after morning. It is God who will heighten our awareness of the oppression and injustice in our societies, whether it is domestic violence, racism or another issue relevant to our own context.

What a challenge it is to be teachers, preachers, pastors and prophets, who remain keenly aware of our daily dependence on God for what we hear and speak. And what an assurance it is too that, when we face times of difficulty and opposition, God is our help and strength.

❓ QUESTIONS

1 What other biblical passages would you refer to in order to learn more about prophetic ministry?

2 What are the obstacles in your context for practising prophetic ministry?

3 What 'sounds' might God be asking you to listen to in your community? How could you speak truth to denial, and hope to despair in these situations?

References and further reading

Linda Belleville, 2000. *Women Leaders and the Church: Three Crucial Questions*. Grand Rapids, MI: Baker Books, 2000.

Walter Brueggemann. *The Prophetic Imagination*. Philadelphia: Fortress Press, 2001.

Walter Brueggemann. *An Introduction to the Old Testament: The Canon and Christian Imagination*. Louisville, KY: Westminster John Knox Press, 2003.

Kwesi A. Dickson. 'He is God because he cares', *International Review of Mission*, 306, pp. 229–37, 1977.

Michael Frost and Alan Hirsch. *The Shaping of Things to Come: Innovation and Mission for the 21st Century Church*. Peabody, MA: Hendrickson, 2003.

Justo González. *The Story of Christianity*. Vol. 2: *The Reformation to the Present Day*. HarperSanFrancisco, 1985.

Frederick Holmgren. *Priests and Prophets: Spirituality and Social Conscience*. Collegeville, MN: Liturgical Press, 2005.

Cheryl J. Sanders. *Ministry at the Margins: The Prophetic Mission of Women, Youth and the Poor*. Downers Grove, IL: InterVarsity Press, 1997.

William Willimon. *Pastor: The Theology and Practice of Ordained Ministry*. Nashville, TN: Abingdon Press, 2002.

W. E. Vine, Merrill F. Unger and William White. *Expository Dictionary of New Testament Words*. Richmond, VA: MacDonald Publishing Co., 1985.

5

Leadership and environment

Dave Bookless

Much writing on Christian leadership starts in the wrong place. It focuses only on leadership within the Church, assuming that leadership is all about how to establish, grow, teach, discipline and direct the Christian community. Lessons are learned from the leadership of Jesus among his disciples, or from the good and bad points of Old Testament leaders such as Moses and David. However, while valuable, this approach misses something very important. It fails to remember that God calls forward people to give leadership not only within but well beyond the community of faith.

Occasionally, as in this volume, there is a wider focus, recognizing that Christ's followers are called to provide leadership beyond the walls of the Church in the wider society. We can think of many biblical examples from prophets such as Elijah, Elisha or Jeremiah who challenged bad leaders and provided a moral lead in their societies, through to political leaders such as Solomon or even the pagan Cyrus, whom God described as 'my servant'. Jesus taught about the 'kingdom of God', a kingdom that includes the Church but also goes beyond it, demonstrating God's kingly leadership throughout human society.

Yet even most 'kingdom' teaching misses something that should provide a foundation for all biblical leadership. Leadership is not only about people. It is not only a call to reflect God's rule in how we treat our fellow human beings. To really understand biblical leadership we need to begin not with a doctrine of the Church or even of humanity, but with a doctrine of Creation. We cannot truly understand what it means to be leaders unless we understand our place as human beings within the wider Creation in which God has placed us.

We will now look at two case studies to see how a biblical theology of our call to leadership within Creation relates to real-life issues.

✳ Mizoram, Northeast India

Squeezed between Bangladesh and Myanmar (Burma) in India's far northeast, Mizoram's geography resembles a corrugated tin roof, with range after range of steep hills and deep valleys – the tail end of the vast Himalayan mountain range. This makes travel and communication difficult – there are no railways that reach Mizoram. There are two other very relevant facts about Mizoram. First, it is 82 per cent virgin forest and part of a unique and still poorly studied global biodiversity hotspot, with extraordinary plant and animal species. Second, over 90 per cent of the state's population are practising Christians, the majority being affiliated to the Mizo Presbyterian Church.

Today the Mizo Church is thriving and powerful, with a strong influence on the government and its policies. It is also highly active in mission, perhaps sending out more cross-cultural missionaries per head of population than anywhere else on Earth, many of them taking senior leadership positions in Christian agencies across India and beyond.

Yet Mizoram has major environmental problems. In the past a fairly small human population was able to depend on hunting wildlife and on a form of slash-and-burn agriculture known as *jhum*. Today things have changed. Hunting has remained popular until recently, despite declining wildlife and the Indian government's policies on wildlife protection. It has been known for pastors to preach the gospel in church on a Sunday morning and then disappear with their gun into the forest to shoot anything that moves. Moreover, with a much larger population, *jhum* farming has become a great problem in Mizoram, with cleared land leading to soil erosion, deforestation and threats to rare wildlife. Now that half the state population lives in the capital, Aizawl, Mizoram is also facing new issues of food supply, demand for consumer products, and a generation of people who no longer remember what it means to depend upon the land for food.

This context of thriving churches, a largely Christian society and yet looming environmental disaster demands some questions:

- What kind of leadership can the Mizo Presbyterian Synod give in the context of a changing environment?
- What does a vision of the kingdom of God in Mizoram today look like?
- With its strong emphasis on mission beyond its own borders, what is the mission of the Mizo Church today within Mizoram itself?

In many ways the answers to these questions cannot be written yet. The Mizo Church is gradually waking up to the Christian understanding that mission includes care of Creation. But 100 years of teaching that focused largely on the human dimensions of the gospel takes time to change. In December 2004, the current author was hugely privileged to speak on 'A Biblical Approach to the Environment', both at a synod of the Presbyterian Church attended by many hundreds of Mizo pastors and also at a seminar organized by the State Department of Environment and Forests. There was a strongly positive response from both of these audiences. At the end of the government conference, an older lady who was forest officer for her village stood up to speak. She spoke of how in the past hunters had been idolized for their skills and prowess in killing wildlife. 'Now this must change,' she said. 'Now we understand that God has made all creatures in love and our task is to protect them, not kill them.' Rather than placing hunters on a pedestal to be revered and respected, she suggested Mizo Christians should be placing those who protect and conserve wildlife on such a pedestal. It was clear that her thinking had undergone a complete transformation as she was exposed to biblical teaching on human leadership within Creation.

Mizoram is typical of a number of areas around the world, where there are thriving Christian communities living in some of the most sensitive, valuable and threatened global 'hotspots' for biodiversity. There is a great opportunity here for leadership, but only if the local churches catch a vision of leadership that includes care for the natural environment.

Mwamba, Kenyan coast

A second, more substantial, case study is found on the coast of Kenya, some 60 miles north of Mombasa. Here amid one of the most significant series of 'Important Biodiversity Areas' (IBAs) in Africa, there is an amazing mosaic of habitats:

Arabuko Sokoke Forest: 30 square miles of forest, the largest remaining fragment of a dry deciduous coastal forest that once stretched thousands of miles from Somalia in the north to Mozambique in the south. As the pressure of human populations has grown in the past 200 years it has been gradually destroyed, along with many of the species that depend on it. Today, Arabuko Sokoke contains six bird species that are near-endemic (found nowhere else on Earth) and various rare mammals ranging from forest elephants to the golden-rumped elephant shrew – identified by the Zoological Society of London as one of the global top-ten species for conservation priority. There are also many butterflies and plants which have hardly been studied or understood. The nearby Dakatcha Woodlands provide another fragment of similarly threatened forest.

Mida Creek and Sabaki River Mouth: a mangrove-filled estuary and river, vitally important for many thousands of migrating and wintering birds, which feed on the crabs and other invertebrates in the inter-tidal mud around the mangroves.

Watamu Marine Reserve: internationally important, yet understudied, reef and sandbanks, containing more than 600 recorded species of fish and several species of turtle breeding on Watamu beach.

There are a number of other important wildlife habitats in the region including the **Tana River Delta** 100 miles to the north, threatened by the proposal to build a 50,000-acre sugar plantation, as well as biofuel and sugar factories.

The local area also contains a growing human population of Muslims and Christians, many of whom depend on subsistence agriculture. Over the past 30 years, many local villagers have illegally chopped down trees in the Arabuko Sokoke Forest, as a source of cash income (often the trees are sold for charcoal production). Sometimes there has been poaching of wildlife too, both for food and to protect crops when wildlife strays outside the forest. Local people say they do not want to destroy the forest or the wildlife, but have no other way of paying for their children's high-school education.

The villagers are not the only human beings in the area, however. The wonderful sandy beach at Watamu, the opportunities for diving and swimming on the reef, and the wildlife in the local forests have led to a growing number of hotels and guest houses. A thriving tourist business provides some local employment but the major profits have been made by foreign companies owning the hotels and tour companies.

In this context, A Rocha Kenya (part of the international Christian environmental movement, A Rocha International <www.arocha.org>) has set up a field-studies centre, called Mwamba ('the rock' in Swahili). Before we look at the practical work that A Rocha Kenya has engaged in, it is worth asking some key questions:

- When there are tensions between the needs of people and the needs of wildlife, how do we respond?
- Where there is severe human poverty, should we use our mission resources for nothing other than directly tackling that poverty?
- What would Jesus want us to do today in Watamu?

A Rocha Kenya began in 1998, inspired by the example of A Rocha International's first project in southern Portugal which started in 1983. The Watamu area was chosen because of the important yet threatened series of wildlife habitats and the lack of long-term conservation research to help with protecting these habitats. A Rocha Kenya's aim was not to impose solutions from outside, but to offer leadership from within, bringing expertise and training, while working alongside local communities.

The team has long-term research and conservation programmes aimed at protecting the Arabuko Sokoke Forest, Mida Creek and Sabaki River Mouth. These programmes involve the detailed monitoring of wildlife, which requires local people to be trained up to record observations and carry out bird-ringing programmes, and staff training for the Kenyan Wildlife Service. All of this activity provides leadership in protecting the wildlife and habitats of the area, but it would be undermined without also addressing the issue of local poverty and deforestation caused by villagers chopping down trees in the Arabuko Sokoke Forest.

In many places around the world, wildlife conservation is in tension with development for poor communities. Conservation organizations have sometimes focused on the threats humans pose to endangered species, but have failed to consider the hardships faced by poor communities. In this case, they might campaign to protect the golden-rumped elephant shrew and other rare species, but would have little interest in how this might affect local people. On the other hand, development organizations, Christian agencies and local churches often try to improve the welfare of people without considering wildlife and biodiversity. In that case, they might seek to provide incomes and education for local people even if these efforts led to a decline in biodiversity. It might even be stated that God has given us Creation for our use (not that of the animals), and that God made human beings to rule over animals, so our needs are more important. Effectively, there is a culture clash between these two world-views, one of which puts the welfare of other species first, while the other puts human welfare first.

What is distinctive about any leadership that Christians can bring into these sorts of situations?

A Rocha's approach in Kenya, and in a growing number of countries around the world, has been to try and avoid this division by holding together the long-term well-being of local people and the ecosystems that support them. As Dr Stella Simiyu, a trustee of A Rocha International and a globally respected Kenyan botanist, says:

> The rural poor depend directly on the natural resource base. This is where their pharmacy is, this is where their supermarket is, this is in fact their fuel station, their power company, their water company. What would happen to you if these things were removed from your local neighbourhood? Therefore we really cannot afford *not* to invest in environmental conservation.

In other words, we should acknowledge that people and ecosystems need to be seen as part of a whole – not in conflict with each other but dependent on each other.

In the Arabuko Sokoke Forest this approach has meant balancing the needs of the local people, who chop down trees to fund their children's education, with the needs of endangered species in the forest. The solution took time to emerge. It came out of building long-term relationships with local villagers, as well as undertaking scientific research on the impacts of human pressure upon wildlife populations. It has led to the establishing of ASSETS, the Arabuko Sokoke Schools and Eco-Tourism Scheme <www.assets-kenya. org>. This scheme encourages responsible eco-tourism both in the Arabuko Sokoke Forest and at Mida Creek for migrant birds, and also tries to ensure that the profits from tourism stay within local communities. It has sought financial support and co-operation from hotels and tour companies in the Watamu area, who have recognized that tackling local poverty and preventing deforestation are vital for the long-term sustainability of their own tourist industry.

As well as these initiatives, individual visitors are told about the needs of the local community. ASSETS runs a scholarship fund, offering bursaries to pay for school fees of children from villages at the edge of the forest. Through gradually growing the scheme from one village to another, it has been possible to monitor the reduction of illegal tree-felling at the forest margins. As a result of the scheme, villagers can now see that their children's futures are best helped not by destroying the forest, but by protecting it. Apart from the bursaries, A Rocha Kenya conducts environmental education in the communities around Arabuko Sokoke and Mida Creek. They use methods such as puppet-theatre presentations, the creation of native tree nurseries in the schools, and they encourage cooking with stoves that require less firewood. In addition, training is provided to enable local people to find employment as guides to the forest and wildlife of Mida Creek. Board-walks and tree-hides have also been constructed, with a small fee payable by tourists, again supporting the work of ASSETS.

The contact between A Rocha Kenya and local communities has led to a greater local awareness of how well-being depends on a good natural environment. It has now spread beyond conservation and environmental education into sustainable agriculture. Many local families were dependent on subsistence agriculture, yet were seeing smaller harvests as lands became subdivided, traditional skills were lost, and soil quality decreased. A Rocha has used a scheme called 'Farming God's Way', a form of conservation agriculture that is much less intensive in terms of artificial inputs (pesticides and fertilizers), but more labour-intensive in terms of seeking to provide mulch and water for individual plants rather than whole fields. Growing the right crops in the right place in the right way has been shown to lead to a substantial increase in yields, reducing poverty and helping local people see how humans need to respect the careful balance within God's Creation.

A Rocha Kenya is an example of Christians taking leadership in an integrated way that involves care for both people and the natural environment. This is a different approach from that of most local churches and of most Christian mission and development agencies. Now we need to turn to Scripture to examine this approach in the light of what the Bible says about Creation, mission and leadership.

Are there important biodiversity areas in your region that are threatened by human activity, where Christians could take a lead in protecting God's Creation?

✳ Genesis 1—2: humanity's leadership role in Creation

The biblical story begins with Creation (Genesis 1—2) and it concludes with new Creation (Revelation 21—22). In between comes the great drama of sin, judgement, law, grace, salvation and the Church's mission, but we must never forget the context in which they all appear. It is a context that is bigger than humanity. It is the context of God and Creation and, within that, of our place in nature, our relationship with the world around us, and our call to take godly leadership of the environment.

The very first biblical passage about leadership is Genesis 1.26–28, and it contains nothing about leadership of people! It is all about the natural environment. These verses are vital in understanding who we are as human beings, and the kind of leadership we should and should not give, because they provide the basis for understanding the relationship between God, people and the world in which we exist.

However, in looking at Genesis 1.26–28, we must begin by admitting that this passage has sometimes been misinterpreted to excuse a deeply destructive – and deeply unbiblical – kind of leadership. Many modern environmentalists accuse Christianity of putting human beings on a pedestal above other creatures, of separating humanity from nature. The most famous example comes in an essay called 'The Historical Roots of our Ecologic Crisis', by the American scientific historian Lynn White, Jr (*Science*, 155, 10 March 1967, pp. 1203–7). White accuses Christianity of being 'the most anthropocentric [man-centred] religion the world has seen'. He argues that theologians as early as Tertullian and Irenaeus in the second century compared Adam, 'made in God's image' (cf. Genesis 1.26), to Christ as the supreme image of God (Colossians 1.15), and they therefore believed that humanity was separate from nature in an almost godlike way. White suggests that before the advent of Christianity most people regarded nature as special – respecting, fearing or even worshipping the trees, creatures and mountains that sustained them – but that Christianity took away nature's sacred qualities, enabling people to exploit it and destroy it. In some ways, the example of the Mizo pastor mentioned above, preaching the gospel in the morning but seeing no contradiction with shooting rare wildlife in the afternoon, is an example of this attitude. His ancestors may well have worshipped nature in some form, and their conversion to Christianity removed this protection of the habitat without replacing it with a respect for all God's creatures.

This belief that Christianity excuses and even promotes environmental destruction has been taught as fact for the past 40 years in many university courses on environmental issues and ecology in the Western world, and has shaped a generation of environmentalists. What is often ignored is that although Lynn White, Jr, found plenty of examples to justify his criticism, his understanding of biblical Christian theology was deeply flawed (as we will see). Also, he believed the solution lay not in rejecting Christianity but in rediscovering other Christian traditions which valued nature – such as the Eastern Orthodox and the Franciscan. He concluded his essay by proposing St Francis as the patron saint of ecologists.

So, what does Genesis 1.26–28 really teach? As this passage is so central to understanding leadership and the environment, and is so often misunderstood, it is worth examining in detail:

26 Then God said, 'Let us make man in our image, in our likeness, and let them rule over the fish of the sea and the birds of the air, over the livestock, over all the earth, and over all the creatures that move along the ground.'

27 So God created man in his own image,
in the image of God he created him;
male and female he created them.

28 God blessed them and said to them, 'Be fruitful and increase in number; fill the earth and subdue it. Rule over the fish of the sea and the birds of the air and over every living creature that moves on the ground.'

The three key terms in this passage that need to be considered are 'image' and 'rule over' in verse 26, and 'subdue' in verse 28.

What does the Bible mean when it says human beings are made 'in God's image' unlike all other creatures?

The term 'image of God' has been interpreted in many ways over the centuries. It has been taken to refer to spiritual or moral awareness, intellectual reason or even physical likeness. All of these faculties are seen to make humans different from other creatures. However, none of these are clear from the passage itself. In Genesis 1.26 God moves straight from creating humankind into giving us a task to fulfil. The image of God is not a title that God bestows because of who we are. It is a function that we are to perform. We are to bear God's image, to be God's image, to 'image God' in ruling over the fish of the sea, the birds of the air, the livestock, the Earth and its creatures. An 'image' is a likeness, imitation or reflection of something. A photograph is an image of something in the real world. A statue is an image of a ruler or god. A mirror reflects an image of the person looking into it. We are to reflect God's image. How? According to Genesis 1, we do this in the way that we rule over the Earth and its creatures.

There is of course (as Tertullian and Irenaeus realized) a connection between humanity as God's image, and Jesus as the 'image of the invisible God' in Colossians 1. However, the link is not that humanity is divinely separate from the rest of nature, but rather that Jesus perfectly demonstrated what it meant to reflect God's image in human form. He showed God's likeness and God's rule in how he related to both people and the wider Creation. Jesus in his human form imaged God perfectly within, and as part of, Creation.

So, if we 'image God' in how we rule over his Creation – in showing environmental leadership – just how should we 'rule over' and 'subdue' the Earth and its creatures?

Some Christians have claimed that we are allowed or even encouraged to dominate the natural environment, and repress it for our own benefit and without regard to its welfare. Certainly, the Hebrew word for 'rule over' (*radah*) suggests an order of relationships based on power. In the Old Testament it is used for the head of a household (Leviticus 25.43) and for the authority of a king's officers over conscripted labourers (1 Kings 5.16). It is used both when Israel's enemies rule (*radah*) over them (Leviticus 26.17) and for Israel's rule over her enemies (1 Kings 4.24). *Radah* in Genesis 1.26–28 is thus clearly about human leadership over and above the natural environment. God has chosen human beings from among his creatures and given us a special role and responsibility in leadership. Yet, the passage does not tell us much about *how* we exert that rule.

Some have also taken the word 'subdue' (*kabas*), in verse 28, and argued that it is a word with violent overtones – of military conquest (Numbers 32.22, 29), of a king forcing his people into slavery (Jeremiah 34.11, 16), and even of rape (Esther 7.8). This would appear to justify the criticism of White and others – by seeming to suggest that God wants us to trample and dominate Creation. However, there are three key things we must bear in mind.

First, while it may be uncomfortable for twenty-first-century people faced with a global environmental crisis to think of humanity exerting strong 'dominion' leadership over nature, we must put both ourselves and this passage into historical and cultural context. Many critics of 'dominion theology' are armchair environmentalists in the urbanized West, who have never farmed the land or grown their own food. For the people of the Old Testament, as for the majority of people in today's world, nature is not simply a beautiful TV programme where only the pretty and harmless wildlife species exist in soft-focus harmony. Adam and Eve were placed in a garden, and gardens require active cultivation and management. Today, living in a world affected by sin and the Fall, we must remember that there is a wildness and brutality about untamed nature. Ruling over and subduing the Earth are things that any farmer knows about. They are the endless task of keeping down the weeds, battling against advancing deserts, or preventing wild animals destroying crops. They include the battle against malarial mosquitoes, tsetse flies, and the parasitic worms which cause bilharzia. There is a righteous sense in which humanity is called to strong 'dominion' leadership in a world of desertification and disease.

Second, Genesis 1.27–28, as we have already seen, is about ruling and subduing in a manner that reflects the image of God. In other words we are to reflect God's character in our dealings with the birds, the fish, the animals and the Earth itself. Once we ask how God exerts his kingship – his rule – over Creation and over people, we find that power and authority are held in balance by love and mercy. Our model of authority over the natural environment is ultimately Jesus, the 'Servant King', who came not to be served but to serve (Matthew 20.28). In Genesis, God declares the whole of Creation 'very good' (1.31), which is not what he would say if he was inviting humanity to destroy and damage it as they pleased! Again and again the

Bible emphasizes that God cares for and sustains the whole of Creation – providing food, drink and shelter for wildlife and farm animals (see, for example, Psalm 104), even in places where no human being has ever been (Job 38.22–27). Reflecting God's image means that our leadership – our rule – is always on behalf of God. Ultimately Creation is not ours – it belongs to God. 'The earth is the LORD's, and everything in it' (Psalm 24.1). Thus our human leadership over nature is delegated by God. We are God's deputies as Creation's stewards, managers or tenants. We are answerable to God as owner for the way in which we use or abuse his world.

Third, Genesis 1 needs to be read in partnership with Genesis 2. These are twin accounts of how God made the world, each giving a different angle on the same basic truths. The two accounts speak of humanity both as part of Creation and also as called apart within Creation. So, in Genesis 1, humankind is made on the sixth day along with all other land animals – we do not get a day to ourselves. Yet humanity is also set apart to bear God's image as we have seen. In Genesis 2, humanity is described as made from the dust of the Earth – emphasizing that we are related to all other creatures and indeed to the Earth itself. Later, Adam is ordered to 'tend' and 'keep' the Garden of Eden, for which the Hebrew text has words meaning 'serve' and 'preserve'. There is thus a tension between our call to leadership (to rule over, subdue, serve and preserve) and our physical nature as part of Creation. We lead not from above, but from within Creation. We are, if you like, leaders within our own family – the Earth family – not some kind of aliens sent to look after a strange planet. It is important to emphasize this strongly, because it has a huge impact on how we manage the environment and use its resources.

Moreover the terms 'serve and preserve' in Genesis 2.15 must be held in balance with the commands of Genesis 1.26–28, to 'rule over' and subdue'. Leadership in its very nature rules and subdues (keeps order), but we are to do this only in a serving and caring way. The word 'serve' or 'tend' is about active careful management for the greater good. It is the work of somebody pruning a fruit tree so that it might be even more fruitful, digging an irrigation channel to protect crops from drought, or even chasing wild animals off a field that is about to be harvested. The word 'preserve' or 'keep' tells us that nature conservation is a Christian calling. We may chase wild animals away from the fields of hungry villagers, but we should avoid killing them without good reason. We are to protect and preserve the biodiversity that God has created. In fact it is a core element of our leadership that we do so.

To conclude this reflection on Genesis 1—2, God's call to Christian leadership is not only within the Church or within society, but within Creation as a whole. Our very first great commission and great commandment in the Bible is the challenge to bear God's image in taking leadership within Creation. We do this humbly, recognizing that we are part of Creation and indeed dependent on God's provision through Creation for all our needs; yet we also lead with the confidence that God has called us and declared us his image.

Does your church have a vision of leadership that includes caring for God's Creation? Describe it or suggest one that could be introduced.

✳ Today's context: crisis in Creation and crisis of leadership

The first few years of the twenty-first century have not been good years for humanity or for the planet. There is overwhelming evidence that human-induced climate change, largely caused by the burning of fossil fuels, is leading to dangerous global temperature rises. These are already beginning to have a devastating impact, especially on many of the world's most vulnerable people and ecosystems. We are already seeing the melting of glaciers worldwide. The consequences for hundreds of millions of people who live in the rain shadow of the Andes or Himalayas will be devastating. Changed rainfall patterns mean farmers in Pakistan, Tanzania or Argentina do not know any more the time to plant or whether the rains will be enough for their crops. More intense weather systems are replacing any regularity to the seasons. There are fluctuations between devastating drought and intense rainfall, leading to flash-flooding and erosion. The future predictions, even from cautious scientists, are truly terrifying unless there is urgent united global action. The chairman of the UN's Intergovernmental Panel on Climate Change, Rajendra Pachauri, declared in early 2008 that, 'If there's no action before 2012, that's too late. What we do in the next two to three years will determine our future. This is the defining moment.'

Yet climate change is not the only problem we face. As I argue in *Planetwise – Dare to Care for God's World*, in many ways it is simply the symptom of a far deeper problem. Even if somebody found a magical, instant solution that absorbed all the CO_2 and other greenhouse gases and an endless, useable clean energy supply, that solution would not begin to solve our environmental problems.

> Climate change is simply the most obvious symptom of a much, much deeper sickness. At the heart of it is this: as human beings we have got our relationship with the planet all wrong. It is not just that populations are growing and energy-hungry lifestyles increasing, but that we have been living in a way that simply cannot continue. We cannot solve this problem simply by better technology and a few hard political choices. It goes deeper than that, right to the heart of who we are. We need to rethink not just how we treat the planet and its creatures, but who on earth we think we are as human beings. (Bookless, 2008, p. 12)

As well as climate change, we are destroying the world's forests at an increasing rate, sending an unprecedented number of species towards extinction. We are using up major resources unsustainably, creating more and more domestic and industrial waste. We are polluting the oceans, skies and soils.

Looking at the Earth from the outside, human beings are behaving like a group of spoilt children left alone in a sweet shop. We are over-consuming things that are not good for us, and hyperactively racing around destroying everything around us. Meanwhile, locked outside the sweet shop are other children who are dying of hunger and thirst.

What are the biggest environmental problems facing your region today?

In this situation, there is a desperate need for leadership. Scientists have provided us with accurate information about what we are doing. They have forecast what will happen and recommended what we can do to adapt and mitigate. Business leaders are, in many cases, waiting for the new structures that will enable them to find productive solutions. Politicians in democratic nations are often aware of the urgency. They are paralysed by fear that the solutions needed are so unpopular that they will not be elected. There is a crisis of confidence in leadership both within and beyond the environmental movement.

We know what is needed and it is going to be painful. It includes abandoning the belief that people in rich nations can continue increasing their wealth year on year without regard to the planet or the world's poor. It includes ceasing to see the Earth's 'resources' as products that are valuable only when they are exploited and consumed. It means starting to see that they have intrinsic value in themselves. For example, a rainforest is today only valuable when it is chopped down for firewood, to grow soya, ranch cattle or produce biofuels. In reality its true value is in regulating the climate, preventing erosion, attracting rain-bearing clouds, and to be overflowing with creatures and plants that can be harvested gradually and sustainably for food, fuel, medicines and many other things. At the heart of the issue is our need to stop seeing ourselves as separate from nature and to remember that we are part of it, completely dependent upon healthy ecosystems for everything from fresh air and water to food and fibre.

Around the world, a variety of unlikely sources, including policy-makers, scientists and environmental campaigners, are recognizing that what is most needed is a moral and spiritual revolution. The influential American environmental writers Michael Shellenberger and Ted Nordhaus state in *The Death of Environmentalism: Global Warming Politics in a Post-Environmental World* (self-published 29 September 2004) that 'environmentalists need to tap into the creative worlds of myth-making, even religion, not to better sell narrow and technical policy proposals, but rather to figure out who we are and who we need to be'. Similarly, speaking both as a globally renowned botanist and as a Christian, Professor Sir Ghillean Prance, formerly Director of the Royal Botanic Gardens at Kew, London, and Chair of Trustees for A Rocha International, writes, 'Science alone will not be able to resolve the situation because it is a moral, spiritual and ethical one requiring major changes in our behaviour. It is vital that Christians enter into the battle to save our planet' (press release for A Rocha <www.arocha.org>, 30 March 2005).

How can the Church give prophetic and practical leadership in tackling these environmental issues?

Part of the difficulty is that many people in the twenty-first century lack confidence that humanity can take the kind of leadership that is needed. If one looks at our record in terms of living in harmony with the planet it is an overwhelmingly poor one, especially in the more 'developed' nations. An increasing number of scientists are talking about Planet Earth surviving the effects of human-induced climate change, but suggesting that humanity will be wiped out in the process. Some even celebrate this, talking of us as 'the virus species' and suggesting that the planet would be better off without us. This is a huge, global, psycho-spiritual crisis.

Biblical pointers to environmental leadership

Our context today is of both multiple environmental crises and a vacuum of leadership. This provides an enormous opportunity for the Christian Church worldwide. As we have seen from Genesis 1—2, we understand that human beings are both part of Creation and also called apart to give leadership within Creation. We know clearly that the root cause of today's environmental problems is a spiritual and moral one. Our disasters are caused by an idolatry of wealth, a greedy overuse of resources, and a failure to acknowledge that this is God's world, not ours. Scripture is clear that Jesus is Lord of Creation – not us: 'All things were created by him and for him. He is before all things, and in him all things hold together' (Colossians 1.16–17).

As Christian leaders today, we need to recover a biblical vision for environmental leadership. As well as the foundations laid in Genesis 1—2, I wish to suggest several biblical insights that can help shape this vision.

1 **Prophetic leadership:** The story of Noah in Genesis 6—9 is far more than a favourite children's story. It has major lessons to teach us about God's priorities for us today. God calls Noah to give leadership at a time of environmental crisis. God shows that he cares about all the species that he has made, not just people, and God calls forth a leader to be involved in protecting biodiversity. Noah is the first great conservationist. It is a role that is prophetic. Noah started talking about the flood when nobody believed there was a problem. Building an ark when there was no rain must have seemed insane, and in today's environmental context God will again be calling some Christians into similarly 'crazy' initiatives. This is

because God gives us a prophetic insight into a future that others cannot perceive.

Today Christian leaders need to be ready to speak out about the scale and urgency of the dangers God's Creation is facing. In some parts of the world there is still denial about this among politicians and business leaders who do not want to see an end to a kind of economic growth based on over-exploiting God's world. There may be corruption that Christian leaders are called to name and expose, even at danger to themselves. In some places Christian leaders may be focusing only on internal issues (arguments within the churches) or eternal issues (as if God does not care about this world). They need the words and actions of a prophetic leader to shock them into facing reality. The role of the prophetic leader is to speak the truth, however inconvenient it is. Passages such as Hosea 4.1–3 powerfully bring home the connections between the breakdown of our relationship with God and our neighbour, and environmental disaster.

2 **Practical leadership:** With Noah, leadership was not just about speaking but about doing – building an ark as well as warning about the flood. Another biblical insight into the practical nature of environmental leadership is in the role of Israel as God's 'light to the nations'. Israelites were not only to worship God but also to model a godly way of living in the land with which they were entrusted. Nearly all of the festivals that God commanded Israel to celebrate were Creation-based festivals, connected to using the land faithfully and declaring that it is God who gives it its fruitfulness. Commands about Sabbath and jubilee were not only about spiritual and social relationships, but also included a Sabbath year for the land and a weekly rest for farm animals. Detailed laws in Deuteronomy and Leviticus about farming practices and animal welfare showed that Israel's role as God's chosen people was to be expressed in how they treated the land – in how they gave environmental leadership.

Today it is equally important that Christian leaders not only talk about environmental issues but also are engaged in practical responses locally and nationally. Examples include the Church of England's 'Shrinking the Footprint' initiative whereby churches have been asked to measure their energy usage and then gradually reduce it. In other parts of the world, churches have taken leadership in encouraging agriculture that takes long-term sustainability and biodiversity protection seriously. This includes reforestation programmes, planting native species which absorb carbon, encouraging biodiversity and providing sustainable fuel and food (through coppicing and replanting, harvesting fruit, nuts, etc.). Organizations such as A Rocha, which now spreads across 18 countries in six continents, also demonstrate practical Christian leadership expressed through local conservation projects. In A Rocha's case these vary from tackling conflict between humans and elephants in India, helping to transform an urban wasteland into a country park and nature reserve in London, and cleaning a polluted river bank in South Africa, to encouraging sustainable bee-keeping in Ghana.

3 **Partnership leadership:** Sometimes Christian leaders are so keen to promote their own church, organization or personal reputation that they will not work with others. Yet the scale of the environmental crises and the fact that they affect every human being regardless of belief mean we should seek common ground. Environmental work provides opportunities for Christians to work alongside those of other faiths and none. While we may disagree on many issues, caring for the Earth is a shared value on which we can co-operate. The biblical call for humans to 'rule over' the Earth was not uniquely given to Christians. It is a Creation command common to all humanity. Sometimes when Christians fail to take leadership, God will raise leaders elsewhere. The biblical example of God choosing King Cyrus is a good one – a pagan leader described as God's 'shepherd' and 'anointed' (Isaiah 44.28; 45.1).

Today Christian leaders should not be afraid of entering into partnership on issues of environmental policy and action. In the UK, secular groups such as Greenpeace, Friends of the Earth and the Royal Society for the Protection of Birds have come together with faith-based organizations (Christian Aid, TEAR Fund, A Rocha UK, and an Islamic charity) to form the 'Stop Climate Chaos' initiative which puts pressure on the UK government to take action on tackling climate change. In these cases, careful discussion and agreement is important. Christian leaders need to be watchful that they are not associated with views and strategies that go against core Christian beliefs. Yet our belief in God as Creator of all humanity and sustainer of Creation means that partnership with those of different beliefs is not only possible but also vital.

4 **Incarnational leadership:** For Christians, our model in leadership should always be Jesus Christ, 'Who, being in very nature God, did not consider equality with God something to be grasped, but made himself nothing, taking the very nature of a servant, being made in human likeness' (Philippians 2.6–7). In terms of our leadership within the environmental area, this has implications both for our attitudes and our lifestyles. We are to see ourselves as part of an interdependent community of creatures, not as lords over nature. Incarnational leadership is also about long-term commitment to particular places and communities. It is about building up understanding of the land, the forests, the rhythms of the seasons and of migration, and then working within those rather than against them. In terms of lifestyle, it means Christian leaders should consider their environmental 'footprint' – the impact their lifestyles have on the Earth and its creatures. We should not be living in huge houses, consuming large amounts of power, driving polluting vehicles. There is a prophetic challenge here to the lifestyles of Western Christians which

is a matter not just of social but of ecological justice. A Rocha's founder, Peter Harris, has spoken of 'the GM (genetically modified) Church, where the DNA of our societies has been patched in, such that the gospel we preach is no longer biblical' (closing address at A Rocha's 'Hope for the Planet' conference, London, 24 November 2005). In terms of practical response, A Rocha UK has set up a lifestyle commitment based on Psalm 24.1, challenging Christians to live as if the Earth is the Lord's, not ours; and to reflect this in simpler, less affluent living.

5 **Integrated leadership:** There is a danger that Christian leaders become obsessed with a single issue to the neglect of the rest of the gospel. In the case of the environment, this could lead to a neglect of other areas of Christian mission, including evangelism, discipleship, alleviating poverty and tackling injustice. Some have created a new environmental legalism where the quality of a person's relationship with God is judged only on how 'green' their behaviour is. Environmental leadership should not be to the neglect of other areas. Yet the greater danger historically has been that Christians so overemphasize the human-centred aspects of leadership that they neglect the wider Creation. That is why it is vital to hold together the 'big picture' of God's purposes in his world. The Bible does that with the Old Testament concept of *shalom* (peace) and the New Testament language of 'the kingdom of God'. *Shalom* is about restoring peaceful relationships throughout God's Creation – peace with God, our neighbour and the environment. Similarly, Jesus' teaching about the kingdom of God is about God's kingship in every area, including the spiritual, social, political and environmental. Taking leadership in caring for Creation should provide the 'big picture' that integrates these elements together. Just as Jesus taught us to pray for God's kingdom to come *on Earth* as in heaven, so we should seek the earthing of God's heavenly rule in our relationship with the Earth and its creatures as well as with our neighbours. Just as Jesus told his disciples to 'Go into all the world and preach the good news to all creation' (Mark 16.15), so we must ensure that we have an integrated understanding of the gospel – the good news – that includes all of Creation

Are there tensions in your region between the needs of the people and the needs of wildlife and the wider environment? Can you suggest some ways forward?

6 **Hopeful leadership:** As we saw earlier, there are many today who are close to despair about the state of the global environment. Some senior scientists believe that whatever we do now, billions of human beings will be killed by drastic environmental disasters and changes. Others believe that we have a small window of opportunity, but that human beings lack the moral capacity to take the necessary hard decisions.

Today Christians have an extraordinary opportunity to provide leadership that is both realistic (taking the problems seriously) and hopeful. This hope is not based solely on human scientific ingenuity or on the power of reformed financial markets. It is based on God's commitment to his Creation, his work in and through Jesus Christ, and his promises in Scripture. In Romans 8, St Paul describes the whole Creation as like a pregnant woman, calling out in agony – a powerful image of our groaning world. Yet Creation's cries are not those of despair but of hope – as with any woman in labour longing for new life to be birthed. Creation is longing to be 'liberated from its bondage to decay and brought into the glorious freedom of the children of God' (Romans 8.21). Through the saving work of Christ's death and resurrection we can have hope not only for the healing of our broken relationship with God but also for the broken and damaged Creation. Just as at the time of Noah God made a covenant promise that included not just people but 'all life on earth' (Genesis 9.17), so through Christ's saving work on the cross all things on Earth as well as in heaven can be reconciled to God (Colossians 1.19–20). That is why we can give hopeful leadership in a time of environmental disaster.

According to Romans 8, Creation is waiting for something else too. In verse 19, 'The creation waits in eager expectation for the sons of God to be revealed.' This is an extraordinary and very important verse. The 'sons of God' refer to all (men and women) who have been re-adopted as God's children through faith in Christ. Why is the Creation waiting for us? It appears that this verse is referring back to the commission in Genesis 1.26–28 at the very beginning of Creation. God designed a world in which human beings were to act as his stewards and servants in ruling gently over the animals and birds, the land and the seas. We have failed in that task and Creation has been groaning as a result. Now the renewing work of Jesus enables us to rediscover that Genesis vision and take up our commission anew. Today the people of God are being recalled to leadership within the environment. This, according to Romans 8, is what the whole of Creation is waiting for.

Conclusion

As we have seen, a biblical vision of leadership must include an environmental dimension. We are responsible as a species for demonstrating God's image in how we relate to and look after God's Creation. In particular, as followers of Jesus Christ, the Creator, Sustainer and Saviour of the Earth, we have a clear calling to give leadership in restoring and renewing the Earth. What this means in practice will vary in our enormously different contexts around the world, but here are some concluding questions that can be applied to each situation and, along with biblical study, discussion and prayerful waiting on God's Spirit, may lead to us recovering our vision that 'the earth will be filled with the knowledge of the glory of the LORD, as the waters cover the sea' (Habakkuk 2.14).

? QUESTIONS

1 If Jesus were to return to your local area today, what would he be saying to the stewards of his Creation?

2 If we are to seek God's kingdom 'on Earth as it is in heaven', what is your vision of the kingdom of God, including environmental transformation, for your area? What are the steps to be taken in realizing this vision in five, 10, 20 years' time? What resources would that need? What leadership role is God calling you to take?

3 How can a vision of caring leadership be encouraged? Perhaps through theological training, printed resources, Bible study materials, videos?

6

Leadership and theological education

Esther Mombo and C. B. Peter

 Introduction

Theological education has a more direct bearing on Christian leadership than perhaps any other single factor. This is because the primary objective of theological institutions worldwide is seen as the equipping and training of church leaders.

This chapter deals with three major issues pertaining to leadership, especially with reference to theological education. These issues are: Church–state relationships, gender concerns, and HIV & AIDS. All three case studies that we reflect on in this chapter are true, involving real persons and real-life situations. In some cases we have changed the names to protect identities, but in most cases even the names are real. All cases represent an East African context of church leadership. We will be using our Kenyan context and our experience of working at St Paul's University, Limuru, to illustrate our desire for change within theological education to better equip Christian leaders. We hope that these examples will help you think of examples of change – needed or achieved – in your own context.

Until quite recently the sole purpose of theological education was to train for ordained ministry. However, in the past 20 years or so, things have changed in several ways. First, there is almost no donor money to support the Church's evangelistic ministry in the developing world. Second, the purpose of theological education is no longer confined to training people for ordination; there is a growing phenomenon of lay pastorate. Third, the training of lay readers has tended to promote the integration of contemporary issues – such as gender, HIV & AIDS, disability, human rights – into theological education. And fourth, there is a growing desire in many countries of the developing world to turn theological seminaries into universities. In Kenya, for example, in the past 20 years almost every major theological institution has become, or is well on the way to becoming, a private chartered university.

This fourfold shift in the paradigm of theological education has had a serious impact on how theological education relates to leadership. Now as chartered universities, many former seminaries in Africa are struggling to produce leaders who can serve in more varied ways than just the ordained ministry of the Church.

 ## The Church–state relationship

There is a glorious galaxy of church leaders worldwide who have heeded their prophetic call and given their life for it. In Uganda we recall in this connection the name of Bishop J. Luwum and in Latin America that of Bishop Oscar Romero. There are others who have suffered at the hands of the state for raising their voices against social, political and economic evils. These leaders include Archbishop Desmond Tutu of South Africa, Bishops David Gitari and Henry Okullu of Kenya, the Revd Timothy Njoya of Kenya, and Fr J. V. Prodhan of India. We believe that theological institutions have an important role to play in preparing ministers to take a courageous and prophetic lead in relations with the state.

> Why should some church leaders suffer at the hands of the authorities and give their lives for the sake of opposing evil in society?

In Kenya the politicians who detest church leaders' criticism of political evils have devised a convenient maxim: 'Leave politics to politicians.' Would the Church be justified in following that maxim? Other politicians, in their bid to defend the status quo, take the interesting route of preaching the Bible back to church leaders. Their favourite text is taken from Paul's Epistle to the Romans: 'Everyone must submit himself to the governing authorities, for there is no authority except that which God has established' (Romans 13.1).

> How are church leaders to interpret Romans 13.1? What are they expected to do when the 'governing authority' appears to contravene God's authority?

The above are profound questions, and require insights from ancient history, the Bible, theology and the history of Christianity. We will briefly demonstrate how students and staff might respond to some of these questions.

From ancient history we learn that there are two streams of thought: God is king; and king is God. The first one was imbedded in the idea of theocracy, and was commonly practised in Mesopotamia and Canaan. In ancient Mesopotamian culture, kingship was attributed to the god Marduk, and in Canaan the high god El was worshipped as king. The second idea (king is God) was enshrined in the religion and culture of ancient Egypt where the pharaoh was worshipped as a god. Indeed the very name of the famous Pharaoh Ramesses means 'Son of the god Ra.' A noteworthy feature of both systems is that the priests enjoyed royal power and ruled with infallible authority on behalf of the king.

In the Old Testament we can see both streams of thought reflected. The Mesopotamian and Canaanite idea of theocracy (God is king) appears to lie behind the so-called Enthronement Psalms (Psalms 47, 93, 95, 97, etc.), which contain the words, 'The Lord is king.' On the other hand the ancient Egyptian idea that king is God appears reflected in the so-called Royal Psalms (Psalms 2, 18, 20, etc.).

But then the Bible does not merely repeat what the people of ancient Mesopotamia, Canaan and Egypt thought and taught. The Bible has its own unique perspective, something that is not found in any other religion or thought. And that unique perspective can be seen in the biblical concept of call and vocation.

This means that, according to the Bible, the power of leaders is not inherited, nor is it a matter of profession. It does not generate itself, nor is it generated of itself (say, by a system of blood dynasties). Indeed, according to the Bible, leadership is a matter of vocation. The power of leaders is conferred upon them by God when they respond to his call. Vocation, therefore, is quite an opposite concept to that of profession. In the professional sense someone may rise up the career ladder on the strength of various personality skills, and by winning competitions. But in the vocational concept great power and responsibility is conferred by God on a person who may be the most undeserving and unskilled. Thus Moses, who needed some speech therapy, was appointed God's mighty spokesman to Pharaoh. David, a mere young shepherd, was anointed to be God's messianic king for ever. Isaiah, the man with unclean lips who dwelt among unholy people, was chosen to see the vision of God's holiness. And in the New Testament Saul the mercenary was appointed the missionary of Christ.

Thus in the vocational concept leadership entails a great sense of accountability to God, and also to the recipients of the leader's services. In the Old Testament we read of two great and powerful leadership offices, those of the king and the priest. At times these two types of leaders are seen wielding absolute power. But in case the power of these leaders became invincible and infallible, there was a third, powerful office in the Old Testament, that of the prophet. God chose and anointed prophets as a unique order of leadership so that they could critique the existing orders of kings and priests, hold them accountable, and thus provide the necessary checks and balances. This explains why prophets in the Old Testament frequently seem to be at loggerheads with both kings and priests, and in return suffer at the hands of these two orders of leadership. Amos was slandered by the priest Amaziah (Amos 7.12–14). Jeremiah was condemned to death by the priests, prophets and officials of Judah (Jeremiah 26.10–16). Elijah was denounced as the 'troubler of Israel' by King Ahab (1 Kings 18.17). And according to a traditional interpretation of Hebrews 11.37, Isaiah was sawn apart while still alive during the reign of King Manasseh.

In the New Testament the three leadership offices of king, priest and prophet are merged in the single office of Jesus Christ, since he is hailed as each of the three at different times. Christ is the king (Matthew 2.2); he is the priest, indeed the high priest (Hebrews 7.26—8.6), and he is the prophet (Luke 7.16). This signifies that the power of all these offices comes from God, and unto God it returns.

During the time of the apostles and in the early history of the Church, the office of Christian priests and bishops was marked by a sense of simplicity and self-denial. But with the declaration of Christianity as the state religion by the Roman Emperor Constantine in the fourth century, Christian bishops and priests began to enjoy infallible powers of the worldly type.

Our interpretation of the Bible suggests the need for the recovery of the prophetic model of church leadership so that church leaders are able to confront other leaders, and the people they are supposed to serve, and hold them accountable before God. Certain courageous bishops belong to such a class of prophetic leaders. Further study of the Bible and Christian history, alongside discussion of the contemporary context, may enable students to stand firm in their convictions when faced with challenging situations.

What does the Bible teach about the relationship between leaders in the Church and state authorities?

Practical pointers

Theological education can build capacity for prophetic leadership by, among other things, a vigorous implementation of the following threefold agenda:

1 **Greater engagement with life outside the Church:** Remembering that the Church exists within the world and the world exists within the Church, theological institutions will need to have much more engagement with the world outside the Church. This would ensure an up-to-date awareness and critical appraisal of contemporary issues. This engagement with the outside world can be achieved by providing more opportunities for theology students and staff to integrate with non-theological institutions, through conferences, sport, cultural events, exchange programmes and reading publications in the secular media. Those institutions could also teach some courses employing non-theological specialists.

2 **Strengthening of alumni inter-relations:** The alumni of a theological institution (indeed, of any institution) can be a great asset in giving feedback about the situation on the ground. Theological institutions there-

fore must strengthen their alumni associations in far more capacities than mere annual general meetings.

3 **Curricular renewal**: Finally, in the light of 1 and 2 above, theological institutions will need to engage continually in revising and renewing curricula. Theological curricula can empower leaders for prophetic ministry within Church–state relations if feedback from the Church, the secular world, theology students and the alumni is fully integrated into the work of curricular revision.

We will now explore this third point of curricular renewal and suggest how it may encourage the appropriate application of biblical, theological and historical studies.

A major challenge for theological institutions in Africa is to devise integrated curricula where the interpretation of church leadership, biblical hermeneutics and appraisal of contemporary issues can all be integrated into a single programme of learning. Such a programme would take into account the question of Church–state relations for leaders, and focus on real-life stories.

At a triennial conference of the Association of Theological Institutions in Eastern Africa in 2003, the Methodist Bishop Prof. Zablon N. Ntahmburi, a leading Kenyan theologian, suggested that it is now time for theological institutions to broaden their curricular focus beyond the traditional courses of biblical studies, theology, religions, church history and pastoralia. They should include the following courses in their curriculum:

1 conflict resolution and peace-building
2 political and economic transformation
3 environmental care and ecology
4 information technology
5 accounting and statistics
6 research methodology
7 human rights and democratization
8 community development
9 gender education
10 interfaith dialogue.

To the above list we might add:

11 integrating HIV & AIDS into theological studies
12 theology and disability studies.

Of particular interest in the above list could be conflict resolution and peace-building, political and economic transformation, and human rights and democratization. The socio-economic and political situation in African countries continues to remain volatile. The Church is almost always viewed as an esteemed mediator. Training of church leaders in such practical skill-based disciplines could equip them better to serve the Church in the wider context of the state. Inclusion of the above broad spectrum of courses into theological curricula would help to equip contemporary church leaders with the necessary skills for managing the day-to-day issues of the modern Church and society. We will later examine two of the issues – gender and HIV & AIDS – demonstrating their relevance in theological curricula.

It seems that theological institutions worldwide are responding to the current need of leadership training, and are now offering newer programmes in leadership skills. The Faculty of Divinity at St Paul's University, Limuru, for example, has recently introduced an extramural programme of study, called 'Diploma in Leadership and Management'. A diploma in management is also offered at Daystar University in Kenya. And there is an Institute for the Study of African Realities at the Nairobi Evangelical Graduate School of Theology in Kenya. Courses on gender, disability, and conflict resolution have already started appearing on the theological education scene, at least at short-course levels. However, that is as far as theological institutions seem to have reached in Kenya. We do not yet seem to have degree-level programmes in leadership training offered by any theological institutions.

This approach poses a challenge for the teachers of 'traditional' curricula (Old Testament, New Testament, systematic theology, church history, religions and missiology).

How do teachers integrate contemporary issues and critical thinking into the fabric of traditional courses – and keep them rooted in Christian values?

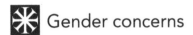 Gender concerns

Case study 1: the true story of Revd Jesca of Kenya

Revd Jesca, an attractive Kenyan woman in her late twenties, had trained for ministry in a local theological college, and after finishing she graduated with a diploma in theology. She was ordained and posted to a parish. She got married and continued to serve the church. While serving in this parish, Jesca became pregnant and gave birth to a baby girl. The parish council allowed Jesca the usual 60-day maternity leave to rest after her delivery. But when Jesca reported back to work after the completion of her leave, there was panic in the church. Both men and women asked if she did not need more time to be away. On the surface it appeared that the members wanted Jesca to rest a little more, but it became clear that they believed she was not yet fully out of the impure state of having a baby, and therefore not ready to take on her role as priest. Jesca was surprised that the parish would hold such views about a young married woman with the potential for having children. She argued that she was now ready to serve the parish, and if she needed more leave she would apply for it. The parish council members appeared to be in a dilemma. How could they compromise the strict laws on purification to allow this woman to carry out her public duties? Why could she not understand this simple matter, that after childbirth she was supposed to be impure? A great debate ensued in the parish council. It took quite a while before Revd Jesca was finally allowed to carry on with her ministerial work.

From the story of Revd Jesca, one is left wondering whether the attitudes shown by the parish council come from traditional African culture, biblical culture or a convenient mixture of both. The story of Jesca is one of many experiences for women who aspire to be leaders in their church, whether they are starting to study theology or seeking ordination, or being made senior leaders in the Church. The issue of women and leadership is becoming increasingly important for a number of reasons. First, women's leadership in secular fields is becoming more and more manifest even if they are challenged in several ways. Second, women are attaining opportunities in education and, in some cases, are even exceeding their male counterparts. As a result of this tendency, religious institutions have begun opening up to the idea of educating women in theology and leadership. But as the story of Revd Jesca shows, discrimination against female leaders continues on the ground.

Can you recall a true story from your own context showing the Church's prejudice against women's ministry?

The move to 'engender'

For a long time, education in theology was exclusively male because it was linked to ordination, and only men were trained and ordained. Women were excluded from theological education because the churches were not ordaining them. Women in some institutions followed programmes which were largely for wives. In such programmes the women were given knowledge in skills that would support their husbands in the ministry. These skills included being good wives and mothers within the home and society. Together with this, the content of theological education was very much oriented towards men, giving rooms only to men for its study. However, with an increasing awareness of the numbers of women in the Church and their involvement in the lay pastorate, the move to 'engender' theological education has gained momentum.

We use the term 'engender' here in a special sense, meaning restoring a gender balance in the education of theology, where both men and women would be given equal opportunity to train for church leadership. A biblical exploration of women's leadership has been given in Chapter 1. That is simply the first step in the engendering process.

The process of engendering theological education means revising the framework and content of the curriculum, and its methods of delivery. It should emphasize the engagement of people in dialogue, their environment, context, faith and what happens in reality. This process enables educators to discern what is normal and unchangeable, and what is contextual and relative. As a result, an engendered model of theological education challenges traditional assumptions in Western theology, African patriarchy and male-centred theology; and instead proposes alternatives that are truly inclusive, affirmative, relevant and fruitful for a meaningful life of faith. Engendering theological education recognizes that theory does not always reflect all practice, and that constructive criticism and reflective questioning are essential tools in theological inquiry and learning. Since theory is often abstracted from particular contexts, true objectivity is not always possible. Therefore engendered theological education stresses conceptuality, dialogue, openness, grace and a willingness to learn and discern God's will in every context.

Open to all

The process of engendering theological education is twofold. First, it is to make theology available to all people at all levels. It is a process that, among other things, seeks to 'demystify' theology by uncoupling it from ordination, and making it accessible to the whole people of God. In contexts such as Kenya, theological education has traditionally been strongly linked to ordination. Only a few people successfully go through the rigorous selection process and take the opportunity of becoming ordained. Even then, gender plays a big role in this process. Female candidates often face tougher interviews. Their call to ministry, their age, their marital status, cultural demands and expectations are scrutinized more thoroughly than in the case of male candidates. Married women, for example, often are expected to prove that their family life, marriage, etc., will not be put under strain by their clerical status. Women who are single, divorced, separated or widowed are often not even considered for theological education on account of the social stigma or cultural inhibitions associated with their status. Financial considerations influence decisions: unmarried women are seen as a risky investment in case they marry elsewhere and leave their dioceses after theological training.

Through the process of engendering theological education, men, who otherwise would not have had an opportunity, and women, regardless of their marital status, are being offered the opportunity to study theology. In this sense theology is truly becoming a study *for* the people of God and *by* the people of God, regardless of their background or cultural baggage.

Reformulating theology

The second aspect of engendering education in theology is to provide the opportunity to clarify theological vision, to reformulate theology and offer a curriculum that is both relevant and life-affirming for both men and women. This process has led to a continuous reviewing of policies and organizational dynamics, as well as evaluating the impact on people's lives in terms of empowerment and transformation. This process, although slow, has certainly helped to increase gender awareness. But it has also raised the level of critical self-assessment and programme assessments in such areas as power analysis, social dynamics and theological critiques of cultural and contextual trends and prejudices.

Theological education can challenge gender inequality and raise women leaders in church society by implementing, among other things, the following points:

1 The cultivation of more funds for female students since women are not equal beneficiaries of resource distribution in most societies, and hence are hindered from acquiring education through lack of funds.

2 Continued engagement with women in ministry by theological institutions. This might be done by organizing special seminars. For example, a few years ago the World Council of Churches (WCC) sponsored a series of women-in-ministry seminars at St Paul's, Limuru, for women leaders.

3 Curricular renewal to integrate more courses on feminist hermeneutics and gender studies. Staff can be encouraged to examine their material and integrate contemporary scholarship into their teaching.

4 Combating the stereotype that says gender studies are only for women. This can be done if both men and women are involved in teaching and learning gender-based programmes.

5 Acquisition of more resources (books, journal subscriptions and other media) on gender studies.

 HIV & AIDS

Case study 2: the true story of Bishop Samuel Ssekkadde of Uganda

The room was heavy with silence. For several long minutes, the two men avoided each other's gaze.

For the Revd Gideon Byamugisha, a priest in the Anglican Diocese of Namirembe, Church of Uganda, the deciding moment had finally come. He had blurted out those four most decisive words of his life, 'Bishop, I am positive.' Revd Byamugisha was facing his bishop in the latter's office. After speaking those words, the tall, lean priest felt a surge of relief. It was over now.

The bishop sat in silence for several minutes. Then he looked at the priest and pondered his strange confession. Finally he spoke in a voice that betrayed episcopal authority and benevolence. 'Positive of what, Gideon?'

The priest by then felt himself recovered enough to reply in a calm, calculated tone, 'I am positive with HIV & AIDS, my lord.'

But to the great surprise of Revd Byamugisha, his bombshell confession failed to elicit any 'bombshell' kind of reaction from his bishop. The old man just sat in silence. Finally, the bishop rose from his chair, walked around, and stood before Gideon. The priest too stood up in a mark of respect that characterizes East Africans. The bishop embraced the priest, and asked him to sit down so that they could pray together.

After the prayer, the bishop began to speak to his priest in a fatherly voice. 'Know what, Gideon? I want to tell you that I am very pleased with your courage and honesty with me. By making that historic confession you have shown the way to millions of men and women here in Africa and in the world who are suffering from HIV & AIDS in silence. I am going to start an HIV & AIDS awareness department in my diocese and appoint you as its director. You will have a car, other facilities, your own budget, and the necessary decision-making powers to run that department.'

The bishop kept his word, and the Revd Gideon Byamugisha became an ambassador of humanity's fight against the stigma and discrimination caused by HIV & AIDS. Eventually the bishop installed Gideon as canon. That was many years ago. Today the impact of Canon Gideon Byamugisha's bold testimony has been felt not only in the whole of Uganda (with a probable contribution to bringing the HIV & AIDS statistics down in that country), but the whole world. He has addressed top world bodies, such as the United Nations and the United States Congress. The canon is living positively in excellent health.

AIDS in the Church?

The most remarkable thing about the above true story is that the bishop who made the radical decision to restore the life of Canon Byamugisha is seldom remembered. He took a bold, radical, loving decision. At a time when the Church was looking at HIV & AIDS as God's just punishment for sinners, the bishop's decision was quite risky for the social image of the Church, at least according to many church leaders at that time. Even now many still look at AIDS as part of God's programme to protect Christian morals.

Around 2003, C. B. Peter experienced this while teaching a class of Kenyan pastors and church leaders undertaking a BA degree in theology in Kenya. When he mentioned that AIDS cases in Kenya had come down from 15 per cent to 7 per cent in recent years, one pastor expressed serious doubts about the truth of such a claim. Soon the class turned into a small discussion group, and students were asked to contribute their views. The outcome was the discovery that many pastors and church leaders in the class had a hidden fear that if AIDS were reduced, and eventually disappeared, then the Church would lose an effective weapon to frighten off morally errant Christians!

When HIV & AIDS first became widely known (at different times in different parts of the world), the first reaction of the Church and its leadership was of denial: 'No, it is not real, and even if it *is* real, it *cannot* be present in the Church. It should be somewhere out there among the sinners. Not here. Not within the Church. The Church is the body of Christ. It is holy. AIDS cannot be in the Church. It is God's punishment for sinners.' Because of such expressive moralizing, the pandemic of HIV & AIDS assumed a highly stigmatized character and was never open to public discussion. Discussing HIV & AIDS in public was just like discussing human sexuality.

The result of the stigmatization of HIV & AIDS was that instead of becoming a problem for medical, socio-economic and spiritual attention, it became a hidden menace, and its victims continued to waste away and die in silence. In Kenya, for example, when someone died of AIDS, the Church happily announced the funeral using the journalistic cliché, 'So-and-so died after a long illness, bravely borne.' And yes, men, women and children continued to bravely bear the 'long illness' and die. The church leadership vehemently opposed any initiatives in HIV & AIDS awareness and family life education. Towards the end of the last millennium, when the government of Kenya sought to introduce family life education into schools, church leaders publicly burnt the curriculum in protest against such an 'immoral' move by the government. At that time HIV statistics in Kenya had hit an all-time high of over 14 per cent, with around 600 people dying of AIDS every day.

How aware of, and involved in, HIV & AIDS-related issues is your local church now?

Mercifully, one of the most delightful gifts of the new millennium has been an almost complete shift in the attitude of church leadership in Kenya towards the issue of HIV & AIDS. What Bishop Samuel Ssekkadde was able to do very courageously many years ago has now been followed by many church leaders.

Today we have HIV & AIDS awareness and education departments in almost all churches (both mainline and alternative). The mention of the pandemic from the pulpit is slowly gaining momentum, and the number of young people constantly visiting VCTs (Voluntary Counselling and Testing programmes) is increasing. HIV & AIDS is even included in family discussions around the dinner table.

The positive result of all this is that the stigma and discrimination associated with HIV & AIDS has been significantly reduced. Statistics show the prevalence of HIV has now come down to about 6 per cent, and the number of AIDS-related deaths has been reduced to some 350 per day. With the reduction of the cost of anti-retroviral treatment, more and more HIV-positive men, women and children are being enabled to live positively, that is, to live healthy, fulfilling and meaningful lives.

What does the Bible say?

And what does the Bible say about Kenya's current HIV & AIDS regime? Many people would be tempted to conclude that, since HIV & AIDS are not directly mentioned in the Bible, this pandemic cannot be included in any biblical reflection. Such an attitude could have been responsible for the earlier, negative response of church leaders towards HIV & AIDS.

But if theological institutions can broaden their hermeneutical scope, they can help students to discover that the Bible does mention diseases which had a great social stigma attached to them. Any medical problems involving skin and blood would result in a social stigma. Thus leprosy (Numbers 12.10), boils of Egypt, tumours, festering sores and the itch (Deuteronomy 28.27) are all mentioned in a negative light, as punishments for sin. Interestingly, there is also the mention of 'wasting disease' (Deuteronomy 28.22), with which the Lord would strike sinners.

Yes, it is true that according to Deuteronomistic thinking (found in the books of Deuteronomy, Joshua, Judges, 1 and 2 Samuel and 1 and 2 Kings), all suffering comes as God's punishment for human sin. But then, one remarkable thing about the biblical witness is that it is holistic, ecumenical and inclusive. The purpose of the Bible is *not* to provide a do-it-yourself manual for religious extremists, but to guide the whole of humanity towards an abundant life in Christ. For this purpose, the Bible almost always presents *both* sides of the coin to provide the necessary checks and balances. Therefore, interpretation of the Bible should also be balanced and inclusive, and no religious extremist should select just a few of the teachings of the Bible, to the exclusion of others, to serve vested interests. We have already seen, in Case Study 1, how some people can interpret some of the biblical texts in their own way to bring about gender oppression. In the context of HIV & AIDS, many church leaders around the world earlier made the mistake of basing their stand on the Deuteronomistic view of history and condemned AIDS sufferers wholesale as sinners, without accepting any moral or vicarious responsibility for their 'sin'. As we have noted above, such a negative and extremist approach badly backfired and the mortal toll of AIDS increased.

What the church leaders eventually seem to have done (thank God!) is to realize that the Bible also presents views of human suffering other than the Deuteronomistic one. According to the significant alternative view, suffering is *not always* a result of sin. Sometimes even good and righteous people suffer equally badly. This view is found in the so-called Wisdom writings, especially the books of Job and Ecclesiastes.

Let us take Job, for example. He was the most righteous and God-fearing man in his age. Job perhaps is the *only* person in the history of the world to whose righteousness God himself testified: 'Have you considered my servant Job? There is no-one on earth like him; he is blameless and upright, a man who fears God and shuns evil' (Job 1.8). And yet Job suffers the fate reserved (according to Deuteronomistic theology) for the worst sinners! He loses all his wealth, his family and finally his health to a wasting skin disease (2.7). This most righteous man of all times ends up on a heap of ashes like a social outcast. He becomes a victim of shame and stigma (19.18–20, etc.), much like many a modern-day AIDS sufferer.

Then there is another view of suffering, according to which the innocent one suffers vicariously on behalf of, and for the salvation of, others. We find this view in the Song of the Suffering Servant (Isaiah 52.13—53.12). Indeed, the suffering and death of Jesus innocently on the cross is a paradigm par excellence of vicarious suffering. In 1990, Louis Farrakhan, the leader of the Nation of Islam movement, acknowledged this in a public lecture at the University of Minnesota when he observed, 'Unmerited suffering is redemptive.'

Finally, there is a view of suffering that regards it as part of God's larger design of the manifestation of his glory. We find this in the narrative of the man born blind (John 9). When the disciples saw the blind man, they asked the Master, 'Who sinned, this man or his parents, that he was born blind?' (John 9.2). This kind of question characterizes the common approach today when we see someone suffering from HIV & AIDS. We immediately associate the medical predicament with sin. Canon Gideon Byamugisha says that when he confesses that he is HIV-positive, many people ask him, 'Oh sorry, Canon. When did you contract this infection? Before getting saved, or afterwards?' But Jesus steers clear of such stereotyping and absolves the man born blind (or even his parents) from any sin and proceeds to heal him so that the 'work of God might be displayed in his life' (John 9.3).

It would seem that church leadership, both inside and outside Africa, has now embraced the holistic interpretation of the Bible to deal with the issue of the contemporary suffering caused by HIV & AIDS. This indeed is a good sign and its good fruits have manifested themselves in the significant reduction of the devastating impact of the AIDS pandemic in our times.

Practical pointers

One of the milestone achievements in the Church's response to the pandemic of HIV & AIDS in the new millennium is a comprehensive programme of integrating these diseases as topics into theological education. In almost all theological institutions (whether conservative, moderate or liberal) the element of HIV & AIDS is generally being integrated in the curriculum these days. Even in non-formal theological education programmes (such as theological education by extension), the HIV & AIDS component is generally integrated.

In the Faculty of Theology at St Paul's University, Limuru, for example, the HIV & AIDS component has a significant curricular presence. While on the one hand, at the BD level, HIV & AIDS is an examinable subject, on the other hand there is a fully fledged Master's programme at St Paul's, entitled 'MA in Community Pastoral Care and HIV & AIDS', delivered under St Paul's

Institute of Lifelong Learning (SPILL). Since its inception in 2003, over 100 professionals have graduated with the MA degree, many of whom are church leaders, including one Anglican bishop. Furthermore, the WCC launched a series of worldwide workshops between 2003 and 2006 with the theme of integrating HIV & AIDS into theological education. Indeed, to help Africa, the WCC has established a department of its own called 'Ecumenical HIV & AIDS Initiatives in Africa'. Thus the current generation of church leaders is receiving theological education with a curriculum element of HIV & AIDS.

The MA programme in Community Pastoral Care and HIV & AIDS, delivered through SPILL, is a unique, practical and broad-based programme. These attributes are evident in several ways. First, unlike most other programmes, the SPILL MA is not designed to launch careers. It does not aim to equip students to get jobs. But it does target professionals and practitioners, many of them leaders inside and outside the Church, and aims to equip them to improve their practice. Second, integrated into the modular curricula are studies of all dimensions related to HIV & AIDS: social, economic, cultural, political, medical and theological. And third, in this programme, there is a statutory emphasis on application of knowledge to real-life situations with a continual two-way feedback between society and the institution in an 'action–reflection–action' dynamic. To achieve this end, each student is required to form a 'base group' in his or her own locality of people who are infected or affected by HIV & AIDS. The base group helps the students to apply their acquired knowledge to real-life situations within the community.

 Conclusion

Prophetic relations in the political arena, gender sensitivity and inclusiveness, and HIV & AIDS pastoral care are just three areas in which Christian ministers, lay and ordained, may be required to give a lead in contemporary society. Renewal of curricula of theological programmes, whether in universities, Bible schools or education by extension, is necessary to provide an informed leadership. Engaged biblical and theological study for appropriate reflective practice will better equip ministers to carry out God's mission. We hope these examples have enabled you to think about theological education in your context, whether you know it as a student or as a teacher. What changes have been made? What further changes could be made to encourage good Christian leadership models? Here are some more questions for further discussion.

❓ QUESTIONS

1 Describe and analyse a true incident from your own context where a church leader (or leaders) came into conflict with the state for the sake of truth and justice.

2 How are the Church and the state related? Should the Church act as an arm of the state, or should it exist to oppose the state whenever the latter breaks God's laws?

3 Explore the curriculum of theological education in your own context and examine to what extent it does, or does not, integrate gender studies.

4 Describe, analyse and critique two true stories from your own context where:

   (a) a church leader showed a judgemental and stigmatizing attitude towards HIV & AIDS;

   (b) a church leader showed a compassionate and pastoral attitude towards HIV & AIDS.

5 Supposing you were a lecturer in a theological institution training leaders for a 'Diploma in Leadership' programme, prepare a course description, course outline and short bibliography for the following courses:

   (a) 'Leading the way for those living with HIV & AIDS'

   (b) 'Women and men: leaders together'

   (c) 'Taking a lead in Church–state relations'.

Conclusion

Titre Ande

I imagine a universal Church with 'a thousand points of light'. Each light is an agent of transformation addressing the public issues of the day, a leader who does not separate conversion of the heart from conversion of society. Our challenge is: how can we make this vision a reality? How can we make Christian leaders effective so they become truly these 'points of light'?

The contributors to this book have responded to different situations in particular ways. We have suggested frameworks for other situations. We have criticized styles of leadership and suggested how we can improve our leadership skills. I hope this book has helped you to think about leadership in your context. In this concluding chapter I'm going to show how my reflection about leadership in the diocese where I am bishop turned into a process of transformative action to change attitudes and actions within the diocese. Then it will be your turn to bring these reflections and your context together for transformative action.

A few years ago I was inspired by a course developed by the Anglican Diocese of Oxford (UK), entitled 'Developing Servant Leaders'. It emphasizes leadership based on a model of service and collaboration which is focused on bringing about change. It examines four key areas in the life of any organization where the leader has responsibility:

- direction (leadership path-finding)
- well-being and team spirit of the people (leadership empowering)
- effective deployment of physical, human and financial resources (leadership aligning)
- leaders' inner qualities and trustworthiness (leadership modelling).

Leadership that does not act in these areas of life will simply maintain the status quo.

The model inspired me to review leadership in the new Diocese of Aru in the Democratic Republic of Congo. Many church leaders had been following the political model outlined in Chapter 2. They led by coercion instead of forming caring relationships. They often tried to control people instead of supporting them. They did all the ministerial functions themselves instead of developing the full participation of all believers, and acknowledging that gifts are given to all by God for service to Christ's body (Ephesians 4.11–13). They acted like selfish bosses of people instead of guiding them like selfless leaders. They often dominated their churches instead of serving in love. They wanted to hold on to their position instead of seeking Christians' growth.

I identified a number of aims:

- a clear sense of direction and purpose for all Christians in the diocese
- a vision that inspired everybody and a purposeful decision-making process
- team spirit among the people in their parishes
- the use of all their gifts and the development of methods of resolving differences of opinion
- the organization of budgets, buildings and people in ways that fit with the purpose and vision of the Church
- leaders with the capacity to analyse and understand the situation, who are ready to commit themselves to be 'points of light'.

What follows is the path we have suggested in the Diocese of Aru for an appropriate leadership in the Church

Think about your own context. How far might the suggestions below be useful in it?

Called and trained leaders

Leadership is not primarily about function, position or talent, but first about gift and call. As Chapter 1 on biblical principles explained, Christian leaders are called by God. Like shepherds of the flock they must care for and nurture others, working with loving servant hearts and without greed. The gift of leadership must benefit from hard work, ongoing reflection, training and maturity. In Aru Diocese we help people to be aware of their call. God's calling and equipping are vital for giving Christian leaders a sense of gratitude, humility and dependence on God. Our local committee for ministerial training selects those who show leadership potential, have a clear call from God to a particular position, are gifted by God with spiritual gifts to fulfil the call, and have the maturity in personal development to continue growing in Christ-likeness.

We encourage the ministry of all believers and commit ourselves to use Christians according to their gifts. We often begin at parish- or local church-level by appointing Christians to lead small groups in the area of their interest to test their gifts. They are selected, empowered and overseen by the local committee and their ministers. Candidates are also free to express their call. If they show good skills and competence in leadership, then the committee sends their names for selection to the diocesan team, which can recommend them to the bishop's office for an appropriate training and effective use.

How do people sense they are being called by God? What processes does your church use for discerning God's call of a person?

We urge church leaders to be anchored to the word of God that gives freshness and relevance in mission. We thus encourage those sensing a call to full-time ministry to complete their schooling so that they have a firm foundation for reflecting upon ministerial practice before they enter specific training. Leaders lay and ordained are enabled in Bible schools or theological colleges to develop creativity, participation and a critical mind. They are also trained through seminars and conferences to question the status quo in the Church and make a critical assessment of the situation. They learn the Bible and develop skills in applying the truths of Scriptures to the theological and practical challenges they face. They are able to interpret new facts and fresh experiences. They are able to integrate their Christian tradition with new ways of thinking so they discern new insights for their faith. They take into account other subjects, such as psychology, anthropology, philosophy and sociology, and link them to the social and development activities in their church because Christian ministers are required to give a lead in contemporary society. As Esther Mombo and C. B. Peter noted in Chapter 6, the curricula of theological programmes in our universities and Bible schools must be renewed to provide an informed leadership. Engaged biblical and theological study for appropriate reflective practice will better equip ministers to carry out God's mission.

Discipleship and mature leadership

The Great Commission as found in Matthew 28.18–20 conceives discipleship to be the end product and natural outcome of global evangelization. This lifelong transformation of converts is based on teaching, not by human wisdom or knowledge, but rather 'teaching them to obey everything I have commanded you'. The divine priority given to teaching makes discipleship imperative for all who respond to the proclamation of the gospel. It is to be transformed into the likeness of Christ as we gaze on him in growing intimacy through prayer, the word and obedience. The higher calling is to become like Christ. When young converts are not steadily nurtured, they become like abandoned babies. The neglect of follow-up to conserve the fruits of evangelism has been the major factor for the prevalence of untaught Christians whose ideas of Christianity are a travesty of biblical discipleship. In Aru Diocese we organize spiritual activities such as prayer groups, house groups, Bible study groups, Alpha course, conferences, retreats and so on, so our Christians are transformed into the likeness of Christ day by day. As Leaderwell Pohsngap underlined in Chapter 3, leaders at each level in our Church take part in the same activities for their lifetime discipleship.

Mature leaders know that leadership is a journey of self-discovery and they have the desire to change as a result of what they learn about themselves. Leaders listen receptively by giving undivided attention to know what the real needs are of those being served. They accept others and have empathy for them as fellow human beings. They develop powers of persuasion and exert a healing influence to resolve difficult personal and organizational situations. They dream great dreams, listen to the prophets and give people a sense of vision. They are committed to the personal, professional and spiritual development of people. They take time to review and reflect before making key decisions. They build a sense of community and know that they are stewards, holding things in trust for the greater good of society and future generations.

In the 1980s, many refugees moved from south Sudan into northeast Congo. They first lived in refugee camps with no relationship with local communities. Revd Onesimus saw the need of the isolated refugees. He started the Anglican Church among them and helped thousands of them to settle in local communities. He built relationships between the locals and refugees, and helped them to live as brothers and sisters in Christ. He valued them all as human beings and built a sense of community among them. He mobilized them to build churches and schools together and to work on small income-generating projects. He promoted the education and well-being of the whole community. He sent people to theological education without discriminating between Congolese and Sudanese. Onesimus was made a canon in the Anglican Church in acknowledgement of his humble service to those in need and the neglected community of the area. The refugees went back in 2003 with good memories of the time they had together, and still keep in contact with the Revd Onesimus and the local Kakwa community. Onesimus is the kind of humble and mature leader needed in our churches to take forward the Lord's mission; mature leaders work practically to fulfil the mission of the Church.

Can you think of someone like Onesimus in your church?

Proclamation and social concern

Leadership within the Church must equip Christians to proclaim the good news of the kingdom set within a holistic understanding of mission. We plant the seeds of the kingdom as we proclaim Jesus Christ and await greater things to be seen in God's time. The world must hear the message of the kingdom, but it will also want to see some concrete demonstration of this message. Jesus' message was demonstrated with power and authority. The Church must make concrete the kingdom of God through tangible expressions of it. The emphasis in Chapters 2 and 4 on prophetic leadership is one of the major concerns of our time and shows some ways of bringing in the kingdom.

Another example comes from Acts 8.6–8. Philip preached the good news of the kingdom of God among the Samaritans with words and works.

> When the crowds heard Philip and saw the miraculous signs he did, they all paid close attention to what he said. With shrieks, evil spirits came out of many, and many paralytics and cripples were healed. So there was great joy in that city.

The proclamation of Christ with words was accompanied with demonstrations of his power, with many signs and wonders. Many people believed and the impact was evident on the whole city.

The Samaritans were considered a marginal community to their Jewish neighbours in Judea. Today we need to consider communities on the margins. We might ourselves be part of those communities. Many Christian communities belong to societies ravaged by poverty, HIV & AIDS, war, and natural disasters such as earthquakes, droughts and storms. We need to proclaim the message faithfully and confidently even amid increasing hostility. The gospel, the power of God, is dynamic for it evolves into newer forms in keeping with each local situation and according to the need of the hour.

As a tangible expression of our proclamation according to the need of the current situation, Christians in the Aru Diocese have set up development programmes for HIV testing and counselling, for community care and orphan support in order to remove the stigma from those infected and affected. In doing so, lay people are involved, both those with medical or development training and those with a desire to support and care for their neighbours. In this action we teach and demonstrate the priesthood of all believers and encourage greater involvement and full participation of lay people in the evangelistic and disciple-making process.

Who do you consider 'marginal' in your society? How do Christians show leadership in their care and empowerment?

In the developing world there is the apparent gap between the widespread profession of faith by a greater number of adherents, and the disproportionate lack of evidence of positive change in society and the environment. Increasing socio-economic challenges call for an intelligent and relevant interface between Christianity and these felt needs. I myself came to understand more deeply that the poor were poor because social structures worked against certain groups of people in a systematic and unjust way. I began to think why my faith had not taken seriously what it meant to work for justice in a practical way and so bring about transformation.

I then began to build Christian awareness by publicly teaching the Bible on social concerns, politics and development issues. It has made the teaching about God attractive. As a leader, I encourage Christians to be part of making positive change in society. With my team I prepare politicians and businessmen to engage their Christian convictions at work. We understand that biblical ethics remains one of the most effective ways of securing social and moral transformation in society. We encourage people to share resources for the benefit of the less privileged. We let people know that Christian mission is not simply about the multiplication of the Church, but to open people's lives to the influence of Christ who gives abundant life. We teach people to think, live and express themselves as followers of Jesus Christ within their specific callings.

We have created a programme called *Ensemble Nous Pouvons* (Together We Can). The programme consists of mobilizing masses of people in the Church and in society to use their potentiality for change. It is a social movement to lobby and effect change. In the Aru Diocese we face many challenges such as corruption, unofficial road-blocks, unemployment, manipulation of poor and young people by politicians for their personal interest, and a lack of infrastructure for education and health care. In all these difficulties the Church can be an agent of social transformation. We have equipped our justice and peace commission together with the Diocesan Development Office to help to understand that development must not be understood solely in economic terms, but in a way that is fully human. The aim must not be simply to raise living standards but to elevate people's sense of human dignity as creations of God, and hence their capacity to respond to God's calling.

As Pope John Paul II said, 'The apex of development is the exercise of the right and duty to seek God, to know him and to live in accordance with that knowledge.' Our leadership is based on the love of God and neighbour. As Mother Teresa said, 'We are not social workers, we do this [working among the sick and dying in the streets] for the love of Jesus.' Understanding these principles empowers us to tackle the everyday injustices in our area.

Environmental responsibility

As Dave Bookless noted in Chapter 5, humans are responsible for the degradation of the life of the Earth. We observe pollution of air, land and water, loss of farmland to erosion, deforestation and habitat destruction and desertification. We have to strive to safeguard the integrity of Creation and sustain and renew the life of the Earth. It is our God-given responsibility to steward and protect the Earth. God's love brings hope for the whole Creation, equipping people everywhere to serve and protect Creation.

How can you show leadership in renewing the life of the Earth?

Members of the Aru diocesan development team visit parishes to lead Bible studies and conferences to explain a Christian understanding of environmental responsibility. They advise villages to clean their public areas and protect their water sources from contamination, thus improving the health of the villagers. They work with subsistence farmers to help them use the Earth sustainably, resting the soil, caring for livestock and replanting a variety of trees when they are used for timber. In doing this they help Christians rethink the scope of the gospel. We understand that environmental work is not simply a method of reaching people, but an integral part of Christian mission.

✳ Salt and light

In conclusion, belief is not enough; now is the time to act. The call comes to us as leaders to play a part in continuing to believe that we can make a difference to the lives of others. We help people to embrace Christ as Saviour and Lord, becoming a living member of his community, the Church; being enlisted into his service of reconciliation, peace and justice on Earth; and being committed to God's purpose of placing all things under the rule of Christ. May we be salt and light in the world.

Index

ND - #0056 - 270325 - C0 - 216/138/9 - PB - 9780281062072 - Gloss Lamination